ZIPPO BOYS

Serving Gay in Vietnam

ZIPPO BOYS

Serving Gay in Vietnam

a memoir

Sydney,
Oct. '19
Thank you for listening to me.

Dave Lara

DAVE LARA

Onward Press

Published in the United States by
Onward Press, an imprint of
United States Veterans Artists Alliance, a 501-C-3 educational non-profit organization.
5284 1/2 Village Green
Los Angeles, CA 90016

www.onwardpress.org
www.usvaa.org

Edited by Christina Hoag
Cover Art by Amy Roberts
Cover design by Teddi Black
Formatted by Megan McCullough

ZIPPO BOYS – Serving Gay in Vietnam by Dave Lara – First Edition

To Gheorghe for giving me life as I started writing this memoir.

And to The Group. You are in my heart forever.

"The difficulty is not so great to die for a friend, but to find a friend worth dying for."

Homer

Some names have been changed to preserve their identities.

CONTENTS

CHAPTER ONE

Weapons of Fire

I wiped the sweat beading on my forehead with my arm and bent on a knee to slice through the mouth of the first Marine. I had to cut along his jaw line from ear to ear then use surgical instruments to break open his mandible, locked in death, to access his teeth. On my clipboard were several sheets of printed drawings that depicted the thirty-two teeth humans are normally born with. On these drawings I indicated fillings, missing molars, crooked cuspids, any unique feature that could help identify the charred remains of the young man lying on the gurney. There was no time to waste. We had had an influx of one hundred and thirty-four dead and one hundred and sixty-one injured from an explosion on the USS *Forrestal*, an aircraft carrier stationed near my hospital ship, the USS *Repose*, off the coast of Vietnam at the end of July, 1967.

I inserted the knife into the jaw and the mandible immediately fell off into my hand.

"Oh my god," I said.

I swallowed and forced my mind to blank out of the horror I felt. I had no idea how many of these mutilations I would be ordered to do. Many of the men had been burned beyond recognition.

"We'll switch off. I'll do the next one," said my buddy Tom.

We'd been assigned graves duty. As Navy corpsmen, we were trained to save men's lives, but we had suddenly become undertakers.

The *Forrestal* had come on station in the Gulf of Tonkin close to Hanoi, the capital of North Vietnam, when the electrical lines on an armed Zuni rocket on a F-4 Phantom jet short-circuited, causing it to fire and strike a fuel tank on an A-4 Skyhawk. Flammable jet fuel spilled across the deck and ignited a fiery, domino line of blasts of other armament and aircraft.

I was dispatched to the *Forrestal* in the dark hours just after midnight, a full thirteen hours ago. My team carried out a final sweep below deck searching for the last of the dead. After we choppered them over to my ship, we began the task of getting these boys home.

We worked all that afternoon and most of the next day, twenty-five hours in total. Besides the teeth plotting, we were tasked with gathering any artifacts with names. I found dog tags, of course, and a liberty card in one guy's pocket. A few men had died of blunt force and wore clothing that had not burned so I carefully cut out name stencils from uniforms. Any items and the oral plotting chart went into an envelope that would accompany the body to the next stage of identity verification.

While we worked, the *Repose* sailed to Da Nang on the southern side of the DMZ. When we arrived, the order went out that all patients and crew were to remain below decks and out of passageways, behind closed doors. The gruesome parade of dead bodies was something Command did not want the crew to see. Those of us who had done the original work were tasked to take the bodies off the ship. The damage to our psyche had already been done.

Several refrigeration trucks waited on the pier, near White Elephant Landing. Teams of Marines stood by to complete the task of placing the dead into the trucks.

As we pulled away from the pier, I stood at the rail outside my ward on A-deck and watched the trucks drive off. Questions ricocheted through my mind. Were those boys green? Had they not done shakedown exercises for deploying live munitions for combat?

I shook it off. The terror in my mind was already headed into one of those little compartments I created in my brain to hold the scenes of the death and suffering I'd witnessed in this fucking war. I hoped they would stay in that Pandora's box of horror.

I sensed someone behind me and turned. KC stood, hands on hips, looking at the same scene. He was a typical southern boy, white and freckled with gangly arms. His eyes slowly moved up and caught mine.

I'd lived in fear of him since New Year's Eve when he'd caught me and another corpsman, Matt, making out in a Hong Kong bar. Drunk like myself, KC beat me up, bloodying my nose and bruising my eye, a gay bashing given to me by my friend and fellow sailor.

"You know, I don't know anything about homos or whatever y'all call yourself," KC said. "I mean, you're supposed to be pansies and pussies and all. Not real men. But cuttin' up those men last night, I fell out after doing three." He looked intently into my eyes. "But that ain't you. I seen what you were doing down there. You musta done twenty or more. You're no goddamn pussy. You're a hero and more of a man then anyone I know."

I stood stunned before I collected my thoughts. "Gay. That's what I call myself. Gay." But he was already walking away.

At that moment I learned that it was possible to get respect, or maybe it was more like validation, from a heterosexual homophobic man. I needed to go above and beyond to prove myself, but acceptance was possible.

It was 1967, and it was a crime to be me.

CHAPTER TWO

What War?

"What's that you have, Stevin?" I asked a buddy of mine one night when we were at our mutual friend Sandy's house in Highland Park, an area northeast of downtown Los Angeles, California.

"Guitar. I'm learning to play. Wanna sing 'If I Had a Hammer'?" Stevin strummed a chord.

Folk music was all over the zeitgeist in 1964, and we knew the words to most of the tunes played at coffee houses and hootenannies at colleges or on beaches. Folk fans were the beginning of the anti-Vietnam war movement, as well as precursors to the hippies.

At that time, we had no idea there was a place in Asia called Vietnam, which we called French Indochina, if we called it anything at all. High school was still a place of innocence. We were unaware that eighteen-year-olds were being conscripted into military service.

So we sang "Hammer" and "Where Have All the Flowers Gone?" and civil rights songs, such as "We Shall Overcome." Steven played simple chords to accompany us. But as teens we didn't know the meaning of what we sang. We still needed to live more life to understand suffering and injustice.

I had a great group of friends that included Stevin, Mara, and three other pals—Tracy, Sandy, and Hank. Others would float in and out, but this was my core posse.

"I'm trying to write music of my own," Stevin said. "It's not finished but here's a taste." He played a beautiful, plaintive tune and sang with emotion in his throat:

> Go to sleep little baby, your daddy's gone away.
> Go to sleep little baby, tomorrow's another day.
> Daddy's gone now, and he ain't coming home.
> Mama couldn't bear it, and now you're alone.
> Sleep on through the wind. Sleep on through the rain.
> You're all alone now and nothing's the same
> Nothing will be the same.

As I realized that my life mirrored the lyrics of this song, sadness overcame me. I wondered if Stevin had felt my loneliness and perhaps by accident, written his thoughts of me. Those words held great meaning for me during high school. They became something like the musical score for that part of the movie of my life. My secret made me feel detached, like I wasn't really living, but instead watching a movie unfold before me.

———◆———

I need to go back to the beginning to get a better understanding of my life.

My mother comes from Spanish Jewish stock. Her ancestors fled Spain probably two centuries years ago to Mexico, migrating to the northernmost part of the country, which was then California. My father is Mexican. His family is from the Jalisco region of Mexico and traces their bloodline to the Huichol Aztecan people. So basically I'm mestizo with a Jewish twist.

My parents met during World War II. My father was in the Army and stationed at Fort Ord in Monterey, California, and my mother worked as a ticket seller at a movie theater in nearby Salinas. After a simple civil wedding near the end of the war, they settled in Castroville, where my mother's family made their home.

My parents were neither religious nor successful. In fact we suffered from extreme poverty throughout my childhood. I knew early that I'd never go to college and because of that, I tried to make high school count. Not academically, but in life experiences.

I looked for interesting things to do the summer before high school. It was 1962. Toby, another friend, and I heard that John F. Kennedy, who was running for President, was going give a speech at the Los Angeles Coliseum. We asked Toby's brother, a city employee, to get us tickets. I wanted to hear Kennedy speak. He was a strong leader who stood up for America both militarily and on social rights. Toby's brother pulled the right strings and wangled tickets for us. We joined a group of high school kids from the L.A. area who had been chosen to go because of academic excellence, although we didn't belong to that category.

We were positioned on the track area of the field, lined up like delegates meeting an important dignitary. I didn't get the meaning of everything Kennedy said, but he was a man who believed in the rights of every citizen—no matter their color or origin. Until this speech, the media and the worldview of the United States was white, privileged, segregated and unconcerned with people who had no opportunity. Maybe the rebuilding of a society post-World War II required that kind of focus but now it was time for change. Kennedy symbolized that change. I wanted to be a part of it and discovered I was interested in politics.

As Kennedy finished, he stepped off the speaker's platform in the center of the football field and walked to a black convertible waiting on the cinder track. He climbed in the back seat and the car drove in front of the stands as close as possible to the crowd. He wanted the cheering attendees to see him up close and as a real man of the people. He rode by our group, and some other boys and I rushed the convertible. As I jogged alongside, I reached out to the president. Kennedy looked at me and shook my hand, using both hands to grasp mine.

Another boy tried to be next, but the convertible sped up and knocked us both back. He was a cute blond kid, and I apologized for bumping him off. He smiled and said it was okay.

Toby was excited by my luck at touching Kennedy. We hugged and danced around. He felt warm and I nuzzled my nose in his neck to smell the sweet scent of his sweat, which I had noticed when the wind blew from the right direction. I had wanted to touch him this way since I'd met him. We had no inhibition in doing this. We'd become good friends.

Toby was a handsome boy with sandy blond hair and the beginnings of biceps and chest muscles. His swagger and manly look belied his age. He knew an older guy, Eddy, who had a black '52 Ford. It was "boss," in the vernacular of the time. Cruising and exploring Los Angeles became the focus of summers all through high school.

Those days were lazy and hazy, as the song went. The 1960s were good to America, and Los Angeles was its center. Our culture was changing, and children were no longer relegated to being seen and not heard. We broke out and lived in ways unheard of in Anytown, USA.

My mother didn't dictate my comings and goings, which included cruising in the Ford through Hollywood late at night. Many parents seemed lax because Toby also had this freedom. We frequented a coffee house called The Fifth Estate, which housed the dying remnants of the Beat Generation. We imagined that we were grown up and sophisticated.

"Wanna smoke? I had Eddy buy me some cigs," Toby said, an unlit cigarette dangling from his lips. His hair hung across his forehead. The streetlights flashed as we drove to Hollywood, making his green-blue eyes especially bright and laughing.

"Cool. I'm going to get some coffee when we get there. Lucky Strikes go good with coffee," I said, hoping I didn't sound as stupid as I felt the moment the words left my mouth.

Toby and I loved going to coffee houses. We listened to beatniks reciting bad poetry or watched Soviet communist propaganda movies like "My Name Is Ivan."

My first year of high school showed me so much about what I wasn't. All the things that a real boy was supposed to like escaped me: sports, academic excellence, popularity, and of course, girlfriends.

I had known since a very young age that I was different from other boys.

When I was five years old, the summer before kindergarten, I worked with my aunts and cousins in a kitchen set up to feed field workers in Castroville. I wasn't much help, but it was cheap childcare, and it was common for young children to bustle about the field hands in farming communities.

It was evening. The men came in from the field and after showering, they shuffled into the chow hall in waves. I was the water boy. I would weave in and out of the long wooden benches and tables that held men and food, replenishing glasses with water from a pitcher. The sound of grumbling and male voices speaking Spanish filled the room as they ate. Then it happened.

I have a vivid memory of having the strongest emotion I'd ever had in my short life. In walked the most handsome Mexican man I'd ever seen. I was not equipped to handle or understand the feelings I had, so I can only leap to the word "love" to describe what I felt.

He had blond, curly hair, white, white skin like an Anglo, and green eyes, which I'd never seen before. He was a wrangling hunk of a man, an obvious *jefe,* a supervisor, as he directed the other field hands. His clothes were just a bit cleaner than theirs. He wore a jaunty red scarf tied into a rakish bow around his neck and the white peasant clothing popular in Mexico. The other men wore dirty jeans with T-shirts or ragged, long-sleeved *camisas* with collars. He was pretty and carried himself with a masculine grace. He stood out from the others.

I stood at the kitchen doorway as he walked by. He stopped and stared at me. I looked adults in the eyes and would hold a strong gaze, which wasn't normal for a child. It was one of the things that made me different. Only when I was being hurt would I cast my eyes down in a defensive posture. Noticing my intense look, he smiled and spoke to me. I don't remember what he said. I shrugged my shoulders in that I-don't-know way that children will do when questioned by a stranger.

He sat at the table opposite the kitchen door and faced me. We watched each other for several minutes, smiling. My Aunt Lucille noticed. Her eyes narrowed and she rushed to me, grabbing my head and spinning me around. She knelt down, scowling disapproval into my eyes and maybe a little fear. She scurried me away, saying something to the blond man over her shoulder. Then summer ended and I started school.

In 1952, we moved from Castroville to Los Angeles. Father's people were centered in San Bernardino, so Los Angeles was more or less in between my parents' families. Soon after moving, my little brother was born. Our family consisted of three children—I had a sister older by ten months and a brother ten years younger —and two parents, the perfect 1950s household, according to the U.S. census.

My father used me as free labor the moment I could walk. Once we moved to LA, he realized I wasn't as typically masculine as other boys and exacted punishment on me with my job assignments. He fancied himself a building contractor and took on odd jobs such as painting for extra cash. It became routine that I would be taken to one of his "jobs" after school and left there until anywhere from nine to eleven at night. At times he made no provisions for food. I would approach the property owner, if they were on site, and ask for an apple or orange. I was always hungry but was embarrassed to ask for real food.

I was very thin as a boy but no one noticed that I might have been dangerously thin. I never said a word about not getting food regularly. I had no trust in adults and was terrified of everyone around me. I prayed every night, "Please let me grow up. I don't want to be a child. Please make this stop."

The insecurity I felt from being outside society's norm caused me problems from day one at school. I flunked many classes, and spent June and July making up my grades in summer school. I didn't really study, but I still learned. Thanks to the repetition of math, English and other subjects, I acquired knowledge.

From the time I was about ten years old, wrestling with my gay feelings turned into a constant struggle every minute of every day. I knew there were men who dressed and acted like women. Once I heard some of my Jewish aunts talking about a cross-dressing entertainer. They made a crass joke when the gentleman joined them for dinner, opining that the chair might disappear up his ass. I knew they were making a sexual innuendo.

American culture deemed these men sinners, damaged or insane. The terror of becoming one of them was inculcated in me by the adults in my life, and I begged God daily to make me straight.

Every so often, we drove north to visit mother's family. Father joined us, but that was because he still had construction work connections in the Salinas Valley. He didn't much like being with us as a family but he couldn't pass up the odd jobs he could pick up, so he would join us, usually driving in a separate car.

In the hills of Monterey were the homes of rich white people. These homes were built of ancient redwoods that money-barons of the 1920s had chopped down, well before environmental controls or oversight. The homes were spectacular, beautiful interiors and exteriors with extensive use of the old-growth trees.

One time in 1960, when I was twelve, I was left by myself to paint a porch at the home of a wonderfully rich person. My father went off to work on the guesthouse at another location on the property. I started with the rails and finished them in quick order. Then I moved to the wall, which I was unaware that, as redwood, was not to be painted. I'd painted about a five by three foot area under the porch window when my father came around the corner with a large pipe wrench in his hand. He saw what I'd done and exploded into a rage, slamming the wrench on the side of my face.

I must have screamed before passing out. When I awoke, a woman was leaning over me. "Don't move. The ambulance will be here soon." She patted me gently as we waited. My father had driven away.

Later, I learned the woman, the owner of the house, had seen the first blow out of the window I'd just painted. If she had not intervened, my father's next blow would have broken my skull and likely killed me.

In those days it was okay to hit children. It was even common for men to discipline women with a slap to the face. No legal proceedings ever ensued.

I saw my father one last time back in Los Angeles. Mother, tired of his constant womanizing and relentless bad temper, had kicked him out. He had packed all his things and was leaving with the last load through the front door. I sat on the living room couch alone, watching him as he walked out. He turned to shut the door.

"I never loved you, David. I know what you're going to become, and I hate you."

By the time I reached high school, my father had been gone several years. The beatings had stopped, but poverty and the burden on my mother of raising three kids by herself made home a sad place. She deteriorated, drinking heavily. Her weight skyrocketed as she overate to compensate for her loneliness and depression.

I worried about her, but I was also worried about myself. I had no real relationship with my two siblings. I dismissed them as ignorant and immature, and worried that I'd have to support them. I shunned responsibility for them, as I was beginning to have dreams of my own. Even though I had mountains of obstacles in front of me, I had hope for a better future.

It was admittedly selfish of me. But I wanted my future and I worried that I'd have to give it to my mother or brother or sister. I didn't like myself for having those thoughts, but if I was discovered to be gay I knew I had no life ahead of me. There was even the real possibility of death. I needed to think of how I would navigate the world. No one else was going to help me, especially not a fag.

I pushed myself to do things that interested me and dragged me out of negative thinking. I took up the clarinet and joined our high school band. There I learned that the Los Angeles Police Department had a youth band. It had a high standard of competence and joining required an audition and a rigorous skill test. I auditioned and was asked to play scales in different keys on my clarinet from memory, which I did.

I passed and became a member of the Los Angeles Police Junior Band in my first year of high school. The band uniforms were the same dark blue material used for LAPD uniforms. We even had police badges, gold braid on our epaulettes, and garrison caps that mimicked the shape of military uniform hats, flat with no brim, hollowed out in the top and pointed front and back.

For parades, we would wear white spats around our black police shoes, which bloused our pants at our ankles.

I looked so good in the police uniform that gay men began to flirt with me. That's how I learned about cruising with my eyes. But there was a lot of pain in my family, and I did not want to be gay.

A camp counselor job that summer and student leadership activities increased my confidence to better myself. Then through an opportunity offered by student leadership programs, I started volunteering as a candy striper at Los Angeles General Hospital. I was the first male in the position, and had no idea how the impact this innocuous volunteer job would have on my life.

While all this activity kept me busy, my secret life reared its head. When I was fifteen years old, Toby and I had sex.

It started the summer before high school. We'd continued being close buddies from junior high. Just before school was to start, he decided he wanted to sleep over at my house in a tent I had set up in my backyard. Our parents agreed, and we gathered flashlights, sleeping bags, and pillows for the campout.

We spent the night talking. "It's going to be cool to be big kids now," Toby said.

"Yeah, it's bitchin' that we got to meet Kennedy and all, plus I think once we get into high school we'll be able to do even more bitchin' things," I said.

After recounting everything we had done that summer, it was time for sleep. Los Angeles summer nights had no real humidity, but they were warm. We spread out our sleeping bags when Toby made a suggestion.

"Let's unzip them completely. We can both sleep on top of yours, and I'll have mine bunched up at our feet. That way we can cover ourselves if it gets cool."

"Good one. These linings are hot so I was thinking I didn't want to crawl into it," I said.

We snuffed out our lights and went to sleep. What happened in that tent still makes for happy dreams to this day. We woke up at dawn facing each other. I looked into his eyes as he looked back, unblinking, then slowly he pulled me toward him, bringing my face to his until our lips brushed. My hand rested on his chest. He had the beginnings of hair, just around his nipples. I had noticed it before, blond, almost invisible, and now I stroked it lightly with my fingertips.

Toby jumped as I brushed his hard nipple. "That feels like electricity," he said in my ear.

I could feel his heart pounding and realized mine was beating at the same rate. After hesitating, I kissed him, a long kiss, and one that I didn't even know how to do. Frightened, we broke it off but we didn't let go of each other. Instinctively, our hands ran down our flanks as we peeled off each other's pajama bottoms and underwear. We knew what we wanted to do. After each dealing with the other's passion, we soon dispatched ourselves with the quickness of young men. We lay quietly together until time made us leave the tent.

A few days later, Toby approached me. "Look, I'm not queer, okay?" he said, half questioning, "and I know you're not either. But if you want to do it again, well, no one needs to know."

I was fine with this idea. I didn't even think men could have an emotional relationship.

At this point the world I lived in considered being gay as not having anything to do with love. "We mustn't kiss like that again either. I mean, that's queer. Okay? Is that okay?" he finished with a pleading voice.

Of course, it was okay. I loved Toby. I just didn't know how to quantify that in my mind. If he thought we weren't queer, then I was okay with that. But I wished he loved me. I wished he would kiss me again.

Our relationship spanned the next two years. We continued to have sex and never had a problem with it. I don't know how he felt, but for me this was the best time of my life. Toby was popular and handsome, and I was very happy to keep our secret.

CHAPTER THREE

Leaving School

Superior Court Judge Roy Ogden presided over family matters, including the status of minors.

"The court finds that we will grant minor, David A. Lara, his request for emancipation based on the following findings: The obtaining of a high school diploma, the petitioner's desire to enlist in the United States Navy, and the court's deposition of the claimant himself. In that deposition we find that the court can apply the mature minor doctrine." He banged his gavel. "So stipulated!"

I stood holding a document the clerk handed me that declared me an adult. I was barely seventeen.

———◆———

It was the time after Kennedy's assassination and I was entering the mid-point of high school. Drums of war were growing louder in French Indochina, and President Lyndon Johnson made speeches about the "American Way" and warned that the communists were coming. We had been living under the "Red Scare" for my entire life. It didn't seem important until the Soviet Union sent missiles to Cuba, and Kennedy stood up to them. But it was still just background noise that I did not stop to think about.

School had special instruction to introduce us to adulthood. The girls had secret, behind-closed-door classes in junior high where they learned about the "little friend" that would visit them once a month.

Boys, especially, were signed up for driving instruction. The classes emphasized defensive driving to try and quell the natural aggression of young men behind the wheel. They even made us watch a horrifying movie called "Signal 30" that showed mangled, twisted bodies of teenage drivers and passengers killed in auto accidents. No censoring, they wanted to scare the bejeezus out of us.

But we were given no information about something that would define every young man's life in the United States in that era. In 1960s America, males were required to register for the draft within five days of their eighteenth birthday. After registering, the Selective Service System would assign him a classification: normal, healthy eighteen-year-olds were classified as I-A, which meant they were available for military service. If they went on to college, they received a student deferment until they graduated, dropped out or were kicked out.

No one sat us down to talk about this reality. There were no civics classes that explained the why and how of this requirement. If you refused to register for the draft, it meant jail time. And you couldn't refuse induction into the military. If the local Selective Service Board picked you, you went.

Because we were in fear of the Soviet Union, questions echoed across our nation about the little problem of growing communism in the world. President Johnson orchestrated an attack on an American gunship that justified expansion of U.S. involvement in the Vietnamese civil war that put U.S. combat troops on their beaches. Some estimates suggest conscription encompassed almost one-third of all eligible men from 1965 to 1969. This group represented those without exemptions or resources to avoid military service.

During the active combat phase, the possibility of avoiding combat by selecting their branch of service and military job led as many as four million out of eleven million eligible men to enlist. But these were volunteers without choice. They were young men who didn't have much other opportunity in life.

This was where my mind settled in 1965, the year before I turned eighteen. College was not in my future, which meant I couldn't earn a deferment. So I made plans to join Navy, so to speak, the moment I left school.

———————•———————

The drama of that year, my senior year in high school, escalated beyond anything I could imagine. The script to the movie of my life was about to take more turns.

Toby dropped a bombshell. We had progressed beyond our years in our physical relationship. We had just finished having great sex one day when he said, "I don't understand why we're doing this, but I know it's wrong." His eyes narrowed and darted away from me. "We need to stop."

I reluctantly agreed with him, but it was a lie. I was gay, and I hated myself, but at least I acknowledged what I was. I felt heartbroken, but there was nothing I could do. He had made it clear from the beginning that he did not feel gay. We drifted apart. We never talked as friends or hung out ever again. I was crushed.

My sister, Ann, became pregnant that summer and a hurried marriage was arranged. Unfortunately, neither she nor the boy was mature enough to rear a child. He belonged to a local gang in the Mexican community next to ours, Boyle Heights. They would both drop out of high school. I wondered how they would support themselves.

At the same time our mother's drinking escalated. The child of an alcoholic becomes the adult in the family when only one parent is around, and that child was me.

Mother would hide the empty pint bottles of vodka all over the house in a pointless attempt at concealing her drinking. I would make a weekly pilgrimage through the house collecting the bottles to throw them away. She had taken up with a man who had been a friend of my father's. One day she ran off with him and we didn't see her for four days.

My brother was seven, and I struggled to make his life normal. I made breakfast and sent him off to school. I scrounged through the alley trashcans for empty soda bottles—they were worth five cents each—to scrape together lunch money, then I would go over to my friend Hank's house and eat dinner. When I left, I asked his mother, Celeste, for any extra food. I would take that home to make sure my brother ate at night. I even stole food from Celeste's refrigerator.

Embarrassment kept me from telling anyone what was happening at home. I started my senior year on shaky ground.

The Police Band was my refuge and an area of real growth for me. I knew there had to be boys like me in the band, but there was no way to find them, especially as I had made efforts to seem "normal." Noticing that some boys in my school were deemed sissy by their walk and hand mannerisms, I had stiffened my gait so my hips didn't sway. I made sure I didn't hold any boy's gaze for fear of them seeing my lust.

But I looked hot in my police uniform, and that gave me surprising opportunities. In fact, I looked so mature that when the Police Band traveled to San Diego for a weekend in 1964 for their Veteran's Day parade, a sailor approached me on the first night. Our band had driven by a bar in a police bus and through the bars of the windows, a flashing neon sign signaled the name: BJ's. The guys made fun of the name as we rode by, but I was curious because I saw young men going in. Later, I managed to sneak away.

It turned out that BJ's was a gay bar. As I stood outside debating whether to go in, a sailor came up to me. I was still in my cop uniform because we'd done some publicity pictures late in the day. We shared some small talk then the sailor propositioned me. "I have a room at the Y. It's only three blocks away."

We knew what we wanted. Toby and I had tried many things that would shock adults. I certainly wasn't naive and stumbling. I had probably gotten more sex than the football captain at my high school.

After our tryst, he introduced himself as I was getting dressed. It was maybe 9:30 pm.

"Hey, my name is Scott and I like you. I mean, you know, want to spend the night?"

"I want to but I have a curfew and they take roll so I gotta get back to my group."

"Wait. What do you mean 'curfew'? How old are you?" He looked worried.

"Seventeen—next month," I said sheepishly.

"Fuck me. You look like a cadet, you know, in training."

I explained about the police band. "How old are you?" I asked.

Scott laughed. "I just turned eighteen, so I guess we're both ahead of the game here. You're not a little boy in the sack, my friend."

He stood from the bed, wrapped his arms around me and kissed me with real passion and affection. "I ship out tomorrow on the Okinawa anyway, early. But I like you. I'm glad we did this."

I finished dressing and gave him a last kiss. "I'm David." I walked back to rejoin my high school group with a bounce in my step.

———— • ————

The final thing that happened in my secret life was a big surprise. My Spanish teacher, Mr. Aguirre, had taken ill, and his replacement was a handsome, white, substitute teacher.

"I will be your sub for the next four to eight weeks until Mr. Aguirre is better. My name is Mr. Clark, and though I don't look Spanish I lived in Mexico for four years."

He was maybe thirty-five-years-old with thinning blond hair. He was an excellent teacher, definitely better than Mr. Aguirre.

I made eye contact with Mr. Clark often. After class, I would meet up with him for whatever reason I could think of although he made me nervous. His age intimidated me, but there was something about him that I connected with.

"You like plays?" Clark asked one afternoon when we went over a test I had done poorly on.

"Yes, some of my friends and I sneak into Hollywood and go to those little playhouses on Fairfax Avenue. I don't get to go as much as I want. The cost, you know?"

He chuckled. "I have tickets for a play on Wednesday. It's in one of those theaters on Fairfax. Want to check it out?"

"Sure. You know the drivers' ed trailer on the other end of the boys' gym? Pick me up there," I said, my mind racing as to what the hell was really going on.

"See you there at seven," he said.

When he picked me up, I was uncomfortable, and it probably showed. We talked about acting and how many plays I had seen.

"I've had drama class twice, so I kinda like acting as well," I said as we drove along Fairfax Avenue. "I've been in about four plays since junior high. I'm not very good because I can't memorize lines very well. It's that studying thing I was telling you about. I'm not a good academic student, even with the things I enjoy, so I've never had the starring role."

Clark said he understood and that I was doing fine, even without the starring role. "You seem to be a smart boy beyond your age. I can see you're picking up on things I and other teachers are giving you. You'll have no problems in life."

The play was boring. Afterward, our conversation tiptoed around what this little "date" was about. "Sorry about the noise tonight. These little theaters have thin walls. Boy, was it loud next door," the teacher said.

"That's okay," I said, "I thought it was sort of funny. I almost asked you if we could duck out of the one we were watching to see what all the noise was about."

"You should have said something. I know it was about war, and it deals with adult ideas and themes. For instance, two soldiers in the play are harassed by the other guys in their platoon for being different and liking each other too much." Clark treated me like I was older. I knew damn well what he was talking about, and he knew it, too.

I insisted that he not drop me at my house. It would be dangerous for him to be seen with me. I knew that an older man with a teen boy could get into big trouble if there was just a hint of wrongdoing, and I wanted to protect him. We sat in the car parked behind the school and talked about plays in general.

Finally, he said, "You know David, I noticed that you're different than the other kids. Do you know what I mean?"

I did, of course, but I was uncomfortable talking about it with an adult. Even if Clark was gay, there was no way I was going to continue this conversation. I became tense. I may have considered myself sophisticated, but who was I really kidding? I just nodded, feeling stupid for not speaking.

Clark laid his hand on my knee. "There are lots of guys like you, you know. Writers from the past like Edward Albee, and Allen Ginsberg and Jack Kerouac are great current writers, and they are all like you. In fact, Kerouac and Ginsberg are lovers. Even some great rulers in history were homosexual, Alexander the Great, for instance."

He'd said the word. Homosexual. I did not imagine it after all, what this date was about.

He continued. "Actors, guys we watch in the movies all the time, are successful and happy despite being gay. Did you know that Cary Grant and Randolph Scott were lovers and lived in Hollywood together? Look at Guy Madison and Rock Hudson. They are handsome men and they are what they are. It's not like people say, that only ugly guys are queer."

He removed his hand from my knee and I tensed, waiting for him to make a move on me.

Instead, he just smiled. "Be okay with it, my friend. It's difficult, I know. I was young once, too. I am here now and I am happy and doing well despite what nature has handed me." He leaned over and kissed me on the cheek. "You okay?"

"Yeah, I'm okay. Thanks. I mean not just for the play. Really, thank you." I stumbled out of the car, half disappointed he'd not made the move and slightly confused.

The world told me all queers, given the chance, would molest me. This man was nothing like that. He spoke to me like a friend. A buddy helping me through a tough time.

At my next Spanish class, Mr. Aguirre was back from sick leave. Clark had known it was his last day.

For the rest of the year I resented Mr. Aguirre but I hated myself less. Clark planted a seed of self-respect in me. He knowingly gave me that gift before leaving.

———— ◆ ————

Mother finally lost her job due to her drinking and her poor general health. Her boss was reluctant, but she was not doing well in any aspect of her life. Then the ground gave way completely. She was forty-eight-years-old, had high blood pressure and probably high cholesterol, too. She never saw a doctor.

I was in drama class when a student worker from the principal's office came in. I became instantly apprehensive.

"David, the vice principal wants to see you in his office," the teacher said.

"Your sister called," Mr. Klinso, the vice principal, said when I entered his office. "She has your brother and is coming for you now. Your mother is in the hospital."

Lance, my little brother, had gone home for lunch and found her unconscious. An ambulance took her to Queen of Angels Hospital. When my sister, brother, and I arrived at the hospital, we were taken to the ICU unit. Lying there, she barely looked like herself. She had been beautiful once, and not in the way that every child thinks his mom is beautiful. She was stunning. Raven hair, thick eyebrows, and porcelain white skin—Rita Hayworth beautiful. Now, she lay suffering from a massive heart attack due to congestive heart failure.

My sister was stunned. My little brother stood confused and frightened. I was seventeen. The doctor attending her asked to speak to me in his office. My interpersonal struggles had made me seem mature.

"Your mother is dead," he said after a few words about heart attacks and oxygen to the brain. "She's only breathing because of the machine. Where is your father?"

I explained that he'd left us a long time ago. When he pressed for more relatives, I told him we were alone. Mother's brothers and sisters were in Salinas and New Jersey.

"I need a decision to be made here," he said. "You want to call someone?"

"No, I'll deal with this," I said. The question was obvious to me. The little experience I'd received working as a candy striper had taught me enough. The doctor wanted to turn off the breathing machine and stop prolonging her life.

"I'll make the decision. Don't do anything until I speak to my brother and sister," I said.

I had already decided we would turn off the machine. As I spoke to my siblings, I was in command. I told them what we would do. I asked my sister if Lance could stay with her until I could figure things out. She agreed.

We returned to our mother's bedside. The doctor and a nurse stood waiting. "Doctor, we'll do what you suggested. How do I turn off the machine?"

He looked into my eyes, clearly hesitant to allow a boy to do that. "I can't let you do that, son. But if you want, stay, and you can be here as I turn off her machine. It may take a while for her breathing to stop. Do you understand?"

It was the only way I could show her I really loved her. I stood by her bedside holding her hand for about ten minutes until she died.

Life had been too harsh for my mother and me to have a real loving relationship. She didn't even know who I was. But I loved her, and the loneliness I would feel for the rest of my life started there. She was gone. We were orphans.

How would I pay the rent? Feed my brother? I was scared out of my mind. It seemed life was slipping away for me just as much as it had for my mother.

I borrowed money from Celeste and Big Hank, Hank's parents, and I received money from my mother's brothers and sisters. With those dollars, I buried my mother and bought a simple headstone. The uncles and aunts came and stood as I knelt at her casket. I stretched my arms across her casket and wept. No one spoke or moved.

Later, Uncle Bobby approached me. "I really don't know you, David. But I have enormous respect for you."

"I'm frightened about my future. I have a secret that could end my life."

"I know. You have a cousin in New Jersey like you. Your life will not be easy. I wish I knew what to say to help you, but really I don't understand why you and your cousin are like that. I do love you but I can't help you. Your aunt will pray for you."

He left with his respect hanging in the air between us. Now what?

My brother went to stay with my sister, but that didn't last long. Our father eventually turned up. He went to her house and took Lance although I didn't see him. Lance was no longer an orphan, but I was.

I had to abandon the apartment and slept on the couch at Hank's house.

"It's only for a short time, I promise," I told Celeste. Her eyes were shiny with tears as she accepted my promise.

With no choice, I quit school. In the meeting with my counselor, he gave me two things. The school decided to give me a high school diploma to show completion.

"There is no point in punishing you. Your instructors have passed you despite the fact you barely get D grades in mandatory classes," he said.

I nodded, embarrassed but grateful.

The next thing he did was give me the name and number of a judge at the child services court downtown. "I already made an appointment for you. Do you understand what I'm trying to do for you?"

The prayer, the chant I had said in my mind since I was seven years-old, suddenly echoed in my head. "Please let me grow up. I want to be an adult."

"I understand," I said.

The counselor continued. "With your diploma, the judge has agreed to issue papers to do something known as emancipating you. That means you'll be considered an adult in the eyes of the law. You will have all the rights as an adult. You can work, join the military, do whatever you want. Do you have any idea of what you'll do?"

"I'll join the Navy, sir," I said flatly. I'd romanticized the Navy ever since a series called "Victory At Sea" was broadcast on television. It showed the heroics of our Navy during World War II. That, and the fact that all my uncles served in World War II and some in Korea, made me always want to join the service.

He smiled. "There's a good chance you won't go to Vietnam. I would've suggested it, if you hadn't thought of that." I stood to leave and he came around the desk and shook my hand. "Good luck, Mr. Lara."

I was an adult. The thing I wanted so badly had come true. I wasn't frightened now. I had a place to go, and like opportunities I found in high school, I would find more in the service. The draft was going to get me anyway. For me, choosing my branch of service gave me control.

My friends put together a picture album of our friendship during high school. It was small and though I didn't know if I could keep it in boot camp, I packed it anyway. Toby and I had dinner on my last night. He said we'd be friends when I returned. "Buddies, nothing more," he said. "Let me give you twenty dollars. I know you have no money. And one last thing, I know who you really are." He kissed me lightly on the lips and said goodbye. He was so sweet.

I promised those that helped me with my mother's funeral expenses that I would pay them back someday. I vowed to myself that I never wanted to be dependent on anyone.

My high school pals Hank, Tracy, and Stevin piled into Mara's VW that Monday morning. She and the gang wanted to take me downtown to the recruiting station. They were really the only family I had. I had already said my goodbyes to my brother and sister and felt a twinge of guilt. Was I abandoning them? But there was really nothing I could do for them. I was just seventeen.

At the recruiting station, I was to catch a bus to boot camp in San Diego. I was happy to be on my way, happier than I'd ever been in my life.

I was in the Navy.

CHAPTER FOUR

I'm in the Navy Now

On the first day of basic training, my company commander ordered us not to join the boot camp choir, which sang at religious services and graduation ceremonies.

"I don't want any goddamn songbirds in my unit, got that men? Got that?"

I did it anyway.

A stereotype of queers back then included choirboys. Hence, the name "songbird." I didn't join the choir to meet other gays but it turned out that was where I found them.

Kip Russell was a boy from Chicago in the tenor section with me. I immediately spotted him as gay and sidled up to him.

"Were you in choir in high school?"

"Yeah, I was," Kip said, "I really liked it, and I got to be in a place where I could be comfortable."

I didn't acknowledge that signal he was trying to give me about being gay. Danger of being discovered lurked everywhere in boot camp. The United States considered homosexuality a criminal offense. In the Navy gays went to federal prison if discovered.

I noted others in the choir who held my eyes for just that moment longer than usual. I stayed clear of them. But I needed someone, so Kip was my boot camp gay pal without confirming it.

27

The choir was really good. The level of singing was high. The civilian director, who was gay, tested each of us for the various parts. He combined harmony and tone that made us sound like a professional chorus, which in reality we were. We performed at different religious services and events aimed at lifting morale.

In the evening after our normal boot camp activities, the choir would march around the parade ground next to the various barracks singing the Navy anthem "Anchors Aweigh." We started humming the tune in unison, then gradually we opened our mouths wide and sang our parts with a full throated "ah ah ah." For the third round of the melody, we broke into the lyrics:

> Anchors away, my boys, anchors aweigh.
> Farewell to college joys.
> We sail at the break of day-ay-ay-ay.
> Through our last night on shore,
> Drink to the foam, until we meet once more.
> Here's wishing you a happy voyage home.
> It was beautiful. I became emotional every time we sang it.

"Listen up, men. The Navy, in its infinite wisdom, has just announced that boot camp is being shortened to nine weeks. The Vietnam War is pumping up. Men are needed and so the rush is on all services to get boots out and doing jobs." As our company commander spoke, we sat like puppies, lapping up whatever he said, although not understanding exactly what it meant.

Nine weeks? I was seventeen and thought that amount of time was huge. On the first day, we'd arrived late at the Naval Training Center in San Diego, and thus learned right away the military concept hurry-up-and-wait. While I had reported for my bus early in the morning, we spent most of the day at the recruiting center in downtown Los Angeles. There was the first round of shots that we would receive before heading south and a few last-minute health questions.

"Are you homosexual or have you ever had sex with another man?" the psych tech asked.

The question didn't surprise me. Men were already trying to get out of the draft. It was common discussion among draft-age boys that claiming you were queer could save you from going to Vietnam, although that was usually followed by howls of "no way" or "I don't want no one to write down I'm queer." So horrible was the label, and by extension the person, that all the young men I talked to about the draft would rather die in Nam than get pegged a queer.

My answer was a quick and unequivocal "no."

I learned that as an adult I would need to hide my true self. Certainly in the U.S. military this would be my reality for the next four years. But by lying, it also made it clear that there was something wrong with me. That realization saddened me. As I entered Navy boot camp, I was suffering a low-grade depression that made me pull inside myself. That, in turn, made me sink into the background. Being unnoticed in boot camp proved an advantage, however.

———◆———

We spent a week quarantined on an island off the coast of San Diego to ensure diseases such as hepatitis or flu didn't get brought into the main boot camp. I was assigned an upper bunk next to an open window that first night. I lay wondering what would happen to me.

At lights out, the camp-wide speakers began to sing "Taps." I cried that first night, partly out of loneliness but also from the understanding that some men and women would soon lose their lives, and "Taps" would be the last song played in their memory.

The next day the company commander passed out books called "The Bluejacket's Manual." We were supposed to memorize just about everything in that damn book, beginning with the Sailor's Creed. The oath stated that I would defend our country, obey orders, and become a "Sailor." When I swore to uphold the Navy's ideals, the legend that I had watched in the TV series "Victory at Sea" became reality for me.

Commitment to the excellence was another ideal. We were tested on everything and were expected to pass those tests or face consequences, formal punishments such as latrine duty or all-night tutoring sessions with the company commander, as well as informal punishments from your own company mates. Each boot's individual results were added together, and the company as a whole was rated on the total. Poor results or failure prompted opprobrium from the company.

I was afraid that my poor study habits would become a problem. I had to put extra effort into studying and memorizing. Despite my handicap, I learned everything they threw at me. Sailor knots, check. Marching, drill exercises with rifle, check. Rowing, boxing, firefighting, check, check, and check. I escaped the fuck-up treatment.

On the fourth night, our company commander came into our barracks for a bull session, which was part of the indoctrination. Ship life was talked about informally with the use of humor and myth. These talks were every bit the same as Morse code training. They were used to form us into a unit and incorporate us into a brotherhood.

I grew happy in this world of men. Sex hadn't occurred to me at this point as so much was being pushed at us both physically and mentally. But as we moved further into military life, the officers knew that would change. The night before we moved off the island and into general boot camp training, the chief and our company commander came into the barracks to shoot the shit.

"Men, we all know a way of stopping the mess of a wet dream is to just take care of it yourself every once in a while." Genial laughing rippled through the men. "So these things will come up more as you become more comfortable here as a boot. I need to caution you on one thing." I could feel the men leaning in collectively. "We all know a strange hand down there makes it feel better when we take charge of these things." More laughter. "Some of you may even be used to having your male cousin help you out every once in a while with these matters." More laughter, although some with a tinge of embarrassment, circled the group. "So here's the caution. That is not the Navy way. You are not to help each other out even a little. As a way to control this, I suggest that at night, when that piss hard-on takes over, just get up and take it to the head. Deal with it quickly and get back in your rack. You night watch guys that are on duty, just leave a man in peace while he's in there and everything will be fine. Your career in the military and in life depends on so many variables. I hope you hear me on this one and act accordingly."

I was stunned. For the chief to give us this talk meant it was common. I became confused. Christians said I was an abomination, a freak of nature. But was I really? It seemed this lecture made it clear that in fact, it must be common. If it indeed was, then doesn't that take away the unnatural part?

I resisted the urge to question some of the cute guys about their cousins. Instead, I turned off the sex part in my head because I was only there to learn and to do a job. Right then and there, I decided that while in boot camp, or on any future ship, I would be at work. I would not allow this personal side of me to interfere with my duty. I don't remember admiring anyone's butt or dick while in boot camp.

———•———

Kip and I drew the same guard duty shift one night. We orbited our barracks over and over, finally stopping at the stairwell for a breather.

"I hate standing midnight watch. It's colossally boring." I laughed.

"You're a funny guy, Lara. I notice you have a side of you that you keep secret. Don't you ever let go?"

"I'm not sure I know what you mean. I don't like that you're hinting that I'm anything like you. It's cool that we share choir but don't think we share anything else."

I cut off the talk with a hostile tone and look. I could see the hurt in Kip's face and eyes. I had just betrayed myself and wounded a nice kid. I did not want to be that guy. But the military put in me fear of discovery that carried huge consequences. Fuck, I hated myself for this, and I lost the respect and friendship of a good man that night because of my fear.

A week later some guys in the chow line called out to Kip.

"Hey songbird, are you queer?"

He cast an eye in my direction. I turned my back on him. I was a songbird. I should have defended him, but I was a coward. Kip would never speak to me again in boot camp.

———•———

Basic training was a game of routine, which began with morning physical training and one to two hours of drill practice. The drill practice got us ready for a demonstration we would perform during our boot graduation ceremony. The whole complement of boot companies took part in a procession consisting of an elaborate display of marching, close order drill, rifle twirling and hat adjustment. It looked great in a grand military display of men in uniform. The Navy band participated, as did the songbirds. Other groups getting advanced schooling at the Naval Training Center also took part as a fill-in to the mass of men on the field. It was all about that special pomp the military is famous for.

I do not say this cynically in any way. I love spectacle. The exhibition served a purpose, too. We became a unit, a military cadre that worked together in perfect unison. It indoctrinated us into military life quite effectively.

Our physical and medical needs were checked, it seemed almost daily. We would have dental work done. Eyes examined, and if needed, we received two pairs of glasses: one clear and one tinted for sun.

One of the men who got glasses for the first time in his life was a straight guy from Alabama named KC Jackson. I got to know him a little during training.

"I love those glasses they gave you," I teased him one night. "They make you look like Clark Kent. No one will ever recognize you for being the dork you really are."

The entire barracks busted out laughing while KC took the ribbing with a shrug. He already had that what-can-you-do-about-it military attitude.

We were being observed in all these activities with notes going into our files to determine suitable job assignments. We also underwent a battery of tests. Some checked for special cognitive abilities. Perhaps you could become the guy that calculated the firing of the big gun on a battleship. They gave us IQ tests to find possible candidates for officer training. I was disappointed to learn I had an IQ of seventy-nine, which went a long way in explaining my lack of success in school. I was simple, but trainable. Others were personality tests to find out things such as whether you could live in the confinement of a submarine and not freak out. In this section, we underwent interview sessions much like the voir-dire used in jury selection.

"What were your hobbies and activities in high school?" asked my interviewer. "Did you do any volunteering for charity or such?"

"I was a candy striper at Los Angeles General Hospital, sort of like an orderly, working on the wards. That was it," I answered.

The man fixed me with a very serious stare and made a precise note in my file that would seal my fate and change my life forever.

The best day in boot camp came near the end. I stood with my legs spread following the directions of the tailor marking my brand new dress blue bellbottoms for sewing. We would wear these for graduation in a week. He tugged at my crotch, and I fought hard not to become excited.

"Okay Boot, do you hang right or left?"

I was taken aback. "I...I...beg your pardon?"

"Do you shove your dick and balls to the left or right, sailor? I have to tailor your blues to hold that stuff comfortable. So which is it?"

Boing! I grew rock hard in his hands as he chalked my crotch. When I stumbled away, I heard him laughing.

I had a regulation bulge to the right of my bellbottom trousers, and I would become sexually excited for the next few months whenever I wore full dress blues. That bulge would grow large on many occasions. I was a proud sailor to say the least.

On the day of our graduation, we were told what our enlisted classification, our job, would be.

I was assigned hospital corpsman, a glorified hospital orderly, not really a nurse and yet sort of a doctor. It was better than being a deck ape on a submarine in the middle of the ocean. I must have had something on the ball for them to send me to three more months of training. I was happy. Hospital work, what could be hard about that?

On graduation day, as a songbird, I did not march with my company but was still part of the spectacle. We sang "Anchors Aweigh" in that very special way, and I loved it. I did feel a little disappointed not to be with the guys in my company. By that time, we were not best friends, but we were a unit—men who were tested and succeeded together. I embraced them wholeheartedly. They were my brothers, and I would forever remember them with fondness and love, so strong was our bond.

After performing the drill spectacle of graduation day, we went immediately to the area where buses waited to take us to airports, Greyhound depots, or train stations. We filed into a courtyard at camp headquarters where our names were read out and orders handed to us about where to report after two weeks liberty.

The scent of men's cologne hung strong in the air with murmurs of "smells like a whorehouse" and "did I put too much on?" as we waited to receive our orders. We all had bought aftershave at the boot PX to go with our bellbottom trousers.

My orders read, "Hospital Corps School, U.S. Naval Hospital, Balboa, San Diego, California." I was to be a hospital corpsman with the rank of E-3.

I said goodbye to the chief and company commander, and for the first time, his voice carried a bit of respect. "Good luck, Corpsman. Good luck."

I had not yet learned the special connotation "corpsman" had in the Navy. But I was proud and anxious to get going.

I had no home to go to spend my two weeks. I had no real family, and my friends had scattered. Some were at college, others were fast becoming hippies. I had nothing in common with them. They seemed childish. I was itching to get back to my world of men. I spent only a week in Los Angeles. Hank's parents put me up again, but I was bored. I cut my liberty short and reported early to Hospital Corps School.

CHAPTER FIVE

Hospital Corps School

An airport taxi dropped me in front of the base chapel, which was situated in front of the Naval Medical Center--Balboa. Pink stucco covered the small house of worship. A large multi-tiered staircase led up to a citadel-like hill. Spread on top of the hill was a handsome Spanish mission revival compound of two- and three-story buildings. Two prominent bell tower-like structures guarded the main entrance. The upper floors had exterior walkways, and elevated bridges connected the buildings, some with rounded Spanish columns. All of them were covered in the same pink stucco as the chapel.

I walked through the passageway between the towers balancing my sea bag over a shoulder and holding a brown envelope containing my orders to report to Corps School in my free hand. I entered a large garden crisscrossed with walkways that meandered between rosebeds, hedges and grassed areas. I passed a large fountain and pond, the happy splashing giving a meditative quality to the area.

Along the walkways hurried nurses in stiff white dresses and caps that held rank insignia of gold and black braids stitched across the lower edge. Patients, mostly men, in powder blue pajamas, drawstring pants, and button tops shuffled by. Over the pajamas they wore thin blue and white-striped robes and on their feet simple cotton slippers.

Some had their heads bandaged or arms in slings. Others hobbled on crutches with their legs in casts. A few hospital beds on wheels dotted the courtyard, patients getting fresh air and sun.

I saw a corpsman sitting on a bench reading, and I approached her to get directions. She was an E5 petty officer in Class A dress blues. The hash mark on her forearm sleeve told me she had been in service for over four years.

I asked her where I could find the Hospital Corps School. She stood and pointed. "Walk through that corridor to the rear of these buildings. You'll see a large cement multi-storied building. That's the main hospital with wards, surgeries, and the main chow hall.

"The main entrance is obvious," she continued. "Go in and follow a long wide hallway to the rear of that building. Continue through and outside there are steps leading down to the Corps School barracks and classrooms. The largest building has the check-in center for new corpsmen."

As I left her, she waved goodbye to me and wished me well.

———◆———

"How many bones are in the human body?" was the first question I was presented with in my anatomy class. The instructor smiled. "You have six days to memorize the names of every bone. At the end of that time, you will be tested."

The training material said there are two hundred and seventy bones in the body. Memorize two hundred and seventy names?

That was only one class. My course load consisted of:

> Patient Care
> First Aid Equipment and Supplies
> Rescue and Transportation
> Emergency Medical Care Procedures/Battlefield Care
> Poisoning, Drug Abuse, and Hazardous Material Exposure
> Pharmacy and Toxicology
> Clinical Laboratory
> Medical Aspects of Chemical, Biological, and Radiological Warfare
> Diet and Nutrition

Emergency Dental Care/Preventive Medicine
Physical Examinations
Health Records
Supply
Administration
Healthcare Administration
Decedent Affairs Program

I was flung into the deep end and had no idea how deep I would sink. KC, my buddy from boot camp, joined me in corps school. While polishing his shoes the first week, he said in his soft southern drawl, "You have to succeed, David. If you don't, you know what happens?"

I shook my head.

"You get orders to an ice cutter in Antarctica, chipping paint and freezing your nuts off." He laughed at his own joke.

As in boot camp, the pressure caused me to learn. I wasn't top of the class, but I learned. I had no time for sex or relationships, but I was never free of lurid thoughts and cravings. However, the social stigma of gayness as unnatural had entered my thinking, making my interior a constant battlefield. I took to drinking too much to quell those lonely nights. I had two buddies who I thought might be gay, but we never mentioned it.

These two friends and I saw "The Sound of Music" five times while on liberty. Sailors? "The Sound of Music"? Really? That was so gay, the three of us should have realized we were sisters.

Sisters became the model I used throughout my enlistment when I encountered other gays. By keeping all gay shipmates at arm's length or thinking of them as sisters, I could stay focused on my job. For me, it was no more difficult to obey than the admonition against fraternization between enlisted men and women officers. If an enlisted man was caught dating a female officer, someone was going to be disciplined.

I used the same mindset that randy enlisted men used to not flirt or try and take out a pretty lieutenant JG nurse. We're not a perfect species, so this strength of conscience did not work every time in either the straight or gay world. But it did work most of the time to allow a well-ordered team of professional men and women, and gays, to work within the military code. Still, I often got so drunk on

3.2 beer at the EM club that my buddies had to drag me back to the barracks and throw me into my rack to sleep it off.

We were a nation at war; underage enlisted men could drink at the EM club. Even on liberty, if you were in full dress uniform, most bartenders would serve you with a wink and a nod. Their attitude was, "If a guy's old enough to go to war, I ain't going to deny him a drink. Tarawa, Guadalcanal, Vietnam? That makes him a man to me."

So a little self-hatred and a strong urge to find someone while on liberty caused me to drown those feelings in alcohol. It was a coping mechanism I would struggle with throughout my twenties.

I succeeded at Corps School. I did minor medical procedures, accurately dispensed drugs for treating the seriously ill, and even assisted with an autopsy.

I was one of thirty boot hospital corpsmen sitting in an amphitheater, watching an autopsy. The chief performing the postmortem wasn't even a corpsman. He was a Boatswain's Mate 1st Class and as salty as the Dead Sea. We all stared in disbelief as he lectured us; no explanation why a deck crew guy was teaching. Our stares included revulsion. He was simultaneously eating a sandwich with a rubber-gloved hand and cutting into a dead body on the autopsy table. He looked up and pointed at me.

"You there, what's your name?"

"HN Lara." I answered, at the same time deciding to skip lunch that day.

"All right HN Lara, get your ass down here and help me remove and weigh the heart."

Remove the heart? Okay, I can do this.

This was a training cadaver, and the chest cavity had already been opened. The chief handed me chest spreaders, clamps and other shiny stainless steel tools. With his instruction I pried open the chest and exposed the heart. Once I'd opened the rib cage, the chief cut away the heart. It needed to be removed intact for study. The chief handed it to me to weigh.

As I carried it to the scales and announced the weight, he clapped his hands sarcastically, causing little bits of flesh and cut bone to flake off. "Well, well, I was sure you would pass out. I'm impressed."

Just then one of my classmates in the gallery did faint, causing the chief to laugh.

"I was hoping you were going to be the first class not to have a casualty, but alas, you disappoint. Okay men, pick him up and take him out. The lesson is concluded. You, HN Lara, wash up. Good work."

I felt myself glowing. How in the hell did that happen? I had just gotten a compliment, a unicorn in the military world.

———————•———————

"Medic," "doc," and "corpsman up" were terms bantered around in conversations that surrounded me at Corps School, although they seemed to have heavy meaning. I was curious how these terms were defined and the context they were used in. I remembered my company commander at boot camp had said in a very serious tone: "Good luck, Corpsman." Finally, stupidly, I asked a group of my classmates what they meant as they were playing cards, a never-ending activity for sailors.

"Lara, are you serious?" Groans and laughter sailed from others. "How old are you?"

"Eighteen."

The guy questioning me was twenty, an old man. His name was Don Amadeo, and he was from New York City, a classy guy who hung out with KC and me for study sessions. He was quick with math, too.

"Holy shit. This guy was seventeen in boot camp," he said to the others. "Fuck, dude, what the hell did you have to do to end up in the Navy at seventeen?"

I didn't answer.

"Well, Hospital-man Lara, let me get you outta them diapers you been in and put you in grown-up skivvies, you shitbird." The men became sober.

Don educated me to the fact that the Marine Corps are technically part of the Navy. "But don't say that to a jarhead." He laughed. "They'll rip you a new asshole. But they got no medics. You're the grunt's medic on the battlefield, Lara, although because we're trained at Corps School, we call ourselves corpsmen. In the military world we have a special status through an Act of Congress signed June 17, 1898. As it turns out, you're probably going to The Fuck. In fact, we were just talking and it seems we are all probably going to end up going to The Fuck."

The Fuck, as it turned out, was Vietnam.

"The word is the president is going all out in Nam," he added.

"That means more corpsmen," another man in the group chimed in. "You, me, him, him, him, are the medics. Why do you think they're jamming us on schooling?"

We had just received word that our training would be speeded up to graduate us a couple of weeks earlier than scheduled. In fact, just two weeks later, we graduated, and of the three graduating classes, two companies received immediate orders to Field Medical Service School (FMSS) training right out of Corps School.

America's military was mobilizing in Vietnam. At the beginning of 1966 some one hundred and eighty-six thousand troops were on the ground. By the end of the year, there would be three hundred and eighty thousand. Escalation would be a word heard in the media over the next five years when speaking about our involvement.

Protests against the draft and the war were ramping up. Cassius Clay (white people had trouble calling him Muhammad Ali) refused to register for the draft, saying, "I have no quarrel with the Viet Cong. No Viet Cong ever called me 'nigger'." In March 1966 groups came together to stage a nationwide protest. They succeeded in getting large numbers of college men and women to demonstrate. In fact, twenty to twenty-five thousand showed up in New York alone, with similar demonstrations held in Boston, Philadelphia, Washington, Chicago, Detroit, San Francisco, and Oklahoma City. Protests also took place in foreign cities, including Ottawa, London, Oslo, Stockholm, and Tokyo.

But I was unaware of these events outside my Navy cocoon. Still young and not really connected to the world, I entered FMSS, a mini-Marine boot camp for corpsmen destined to join units in battle, at Camp Pendleton in Oceanside, just north of San Diego.

The purpose of the FMSS was to learn medical techniques used in combat conditions. It was also a bonding exercise, which was important. Both the Marines and the Navy worked at the school to develop a working bond since sailors and Marines usually don't get along.

The camp was filled to capacity with men being trained to deploy directly to Vietnam, so my group of corpsmen was housed in temporary billets in an area near Edison Chapel. We called it "Camp Edison." From our barracks on the second floor, we could see the main freeway connecting Los Angeles to San Diego. Beyond that lay the Pacific Ocean. Nothing else but empty fields of four-foot high chaparral and a bunch of jackrabbits surrounded us.

I became a member of the 1st Marine Division. "Shit, this is not what I signed up for," I said to no one as I stepped off the bus.

Area 21, Camp Del Mar, was the home of "Marine Expeditionary Force Headquarters, Field Medical Training Battalion," as declared by the sign hanging over the XO's office. I remembered my recent conversation with Don and thought, "Holy shit, I really am going to The Fuck!"

Don and KC were already checked in. I found them in the barracks.

"What's up?" I asked.

KC spoke in a whisper. "The jarheads are giving us a bit of attitude. They're just boots like us so pay them no mind."

They disappeared to inspect the area with the promise of reporting back when they found the chow hall. As I unpacked, a PFC Marine walked in and took his rack assignment five bunks away from me.

"I hear corpsmen are all fags. You a fag?" he spit out as he passed. He laughed.

I felt like vomiting. Was I so obvious? Even if there was no real evidence of someone being gay, in the military just the accusation caused investigations and interrogations that the Spanish Inquisition would have been proud of. I calmed myself with arguments that I'd been using for a long time. I wasn't waving my hands around like a girl. I had stiffened my gait to the point of having my butt ache all day long. No, this was just a jerk, I decided. He was not really reading me as gay. I ignored him.

His name was Cliff, and he was one of those short fuckers the Marines seemed to like to recruit, maybe five foot two, all buzz cut reg. I couldn't tell by his speech where he was from. He sounded like one of those people on television who seem to have no accent. I guessed he was from somewhere in Midwest.

I took to calling him Asshole Cliff, behind his back of course. I hoped he would learn that I could be his lifeline someday so it was best not to piss me off or he could lose out in the end.

I soon became a cog in the "green machine," the Marine Corps. Marine training was intense and serious. There were things we learned that could save our lives and the lives of those we fought with. I paid attention like I had never done in my life.

———— ◆ ————

At Camp Edison, where I became part of USMC operating forces, I trained with my pals. When finished, I would be a Field Medical Service Technician, NEC designation 8404.

The Geneva Convention states battlefield medical personnel are exempt from enemy fire. By that agreement, a corpsman was not allowed to carry an M-16, grenades, flamethrowers or any combat weapon other than a .45 pistol.

I qualified for my pistol on the range at Pendleton. Holding the now-hot piece in my hand after my qualifying round, I couldn't help wondering if I would have to turn the pistol to my own head someday. Being a prisoner of war was something I wanted to avoid.

I was provided with specialized training in advanced emergency medicine and the fundamentals of Marine Corps life. This included physical conditioning, and basic battlefield tactics, field-of-fire being an important one.

"Men!" our drill instructor shouted. "Today you will be operating under simulated firefight conditions. The rounds going off around you are not live, but you must operate in this exercise as if they are real. My team and I will train you on procedures for moving wounded Marines in a firefight situation to waiting Hueys. Marines, you will be operating with blank munitions in the practice of proper field-of-fire procedures."

A senior corpsman was assigned to guide Don, KC, me and a dozen other corpsmen in the training.

"Corpsmen up!" he shouted. We gathered around him where he stood over a prone Marine in front of him. "KC, come forward and get down on your knees above his head. Now, L-T," he said as separate letters, "has designated the field-of-fire as going from that rock outcropping to that stand of trees over there."

He was pointing north and west, using his arms to make a V shape. "Because you're exposed here, you need to get down on your backside. Sit your ass down on your butt, KC."

KC dropped to the ground with his legs almost wrapping the Marine's head.

"Lean over and put your arms under his armpits then push like hell with your heels and leg muscles, going south toward the choppers. Stay out of the invisible triangle formed by the rocks and trees. Got that?"

As the firefight started, it was obvious that any torso or head rising above three feet in the area where men were shooting would get a man killed.

Next we learned that if the wounded guy was awake and able, then we had him lie on his back, reach up to hug our neck in a lovers' embrace as the corpsman crab-crawled out of the flying bullets.

"Your final test will be a full-on dead-man lift-and-carry. The term refers to the fact that an unconscious man is dead weight. We want you to learn techniques that allow even a small man to lift and carry someone out in a hurry."

We stood in a semi-circle watching as our instructor took one of the heavier boys and laid him on the ground. "If your unconscious man is on his stomach, turn him over and spread his arms out. Then you turn around and lay your back on his stomach." He went on to demonstrate a complicated technique of taking the wounded soldier's arm and placing it around your neck and chest. Then with your leg, same side as the patient's arm, you throw it to your opposite side and get to an upright squatting position, one of your legs supporting all the weight. "Finally, use your legs to get into a standing position. Carry your man until you become exhausted and pass him to another grunt. I'll demonstrate how that's done later. This takes practice, so we will be spending all day with you men doing it over and over. Understand?"

We all gave a Marine grunt of acknowledgement and practiced. I weighed just a hundred and twenty-five pounds but I did it. Despite the trainer's attempt to sanitize the name of this procedure, I soberly understood this technique would be use to remove our dead from the battlefield.

It was an exhausting day. At the end the instructor stood before the complement of corpsmen and Marines. "All right, you corpsmen. About the only man to perform well was Lara. You get an 'atta-boy' entered in your file, Mister. The rest of you, more opportunities to improve will come."

He continued with his talk directed to the Marines and what they had just done in the exercise. I looked over to Asshole Cliff. He was smirking at me, twisting his mouth to the side. He spoke to the man next to him. I could read his lips, and I easily interpreted "fag." I narrowed my eyes at him. I wanted him to know that he was not fooling me with his secret war against me.

KC slapped my back as we broke ranks, "You kiss-ass Lara. You done outdid us all. Way to go, man. Way to go."

I felt good. Despite Asshole Cliff and KC's sarcasm, I had won mutual respect from and formed a bond with Marines in my company through hard work and performance. That included my fellow corpsmen. I continually performed well in front of them.

Medical training continued, but it became more specific for field conditions. Stopping bleeding, clearing airways, splinting fractured bones with material on hand. Improvise, adapt, and do what you could with the things in your kit.

A couple of times we went up to the Naval Hospital at Balboa for more advanced procedure training. We became proficient in drawing blood by working in the blood bank. We started IVs on real patients at the hospital. Removing debris from wounds, suturing and complex procedures were taught to us in the emergency room of the Naval Hospital. I learned to draw blood from the femoral artery located deep in the tissue of the inner thigh. I learned to do a cut-down, a surgical procedure used to start an IV when unable to locate a surface vein in a badly wounded Marine. This was an extreme procedure, which was normally left to a trained physician. Yet, here I was, a boy, really, learning to be sort-of-a-doctor.

Our training included several movies showing combat Army medics and Navy corpsmen in action. The films showed us what was done to rehabilitate men wounded in war and some outcomes for the patients who had been saved. These films were extremely graphic.

One in particular was a film from the Korean War, which was still up-to-date for medical practices then. This movie showed what extremely wounded men go through during the recovery process. One guy was a triple amputee, blind, missing an ear, and with a plate replacing part of the skull that had been blown away. He was also missing his balls and dick. I was shocked that he'd lived. I couldn't help but feel appalled that they had saved him. Life did not appear ideal for that young man. Unlike the feel-good documentaries of today, where we show family and community behind the wounded man, this movie showed just the facts of the medical case. No back story. We had no idea what became of him. He kept breathing. That was all that mattered.

There were several of these films showing faces half-blown away, legless men made mobile by rolling on pallets, men with permanent colostomies. The images were grueling, and it was difficult to sleep afterward.

Part of our training included necessary propaganda. We were taught that the Vietnamese were not like regular humans. They did not perceive life like us. They did not mourn death like us. Dehumanizing our enemy went so far as to claim they had no human emotions. In a way, it was true. The communist government of North Vietnam had put a bounty on every corpsman killed in action. So Charlie was always looking for us to make an extra buck. We had to be prepared.

———— • ————

Near the end of training I pulled midnight duty at the aid station located on base at Pendleton. It was just me and a doctor who had recently returned from Vietnam. At around 0100, we received a call from the main gate that an ambulance was coming in with a Marine who had cut his arm while at a bar in nearby Vista. The civilian ambulance rolled in, and two drivers brought in a guy with blood-soaked bandages wrapped around his left arm.

It was Asshole Cliff. As he rolled by, pain showed on his face and his eyes locked on mine. The doctor bent over Cliff and removed the bandages as I turned away to get a suture kit, Novocain and saline water. I already knew what was needed.

"It's not too bad," the doc said. "Bleeding pretty much controlled. We'll get you sewn up quick, Marine, don't worry. Let me go scrub up a bit." He left, and I turned back to set up a table and tray to hold what the doctor would need.

Cliff appeared worried. He looked me straight in the eyes and said quietly, "Lara, don't let that doc work on me."

"You need cleaning up and some sutures. What's wrong?"

"I think he's drunk or at least really hung over. When he removed my bandages, his breath was a hundred proof and his hands shook like crazy. Please, Lara, can you work on me?"

Asshole Cliff was asking for my help.

We stared at each other for a few tense seconds. Finally, I nodded and left the room to speak to the doctor.

"That was easy," I said as I returned. "He says he's tired and thanked me big time for offering to suture you up. You're right. He was on a bender last night. The cloud of booze breath was strong around his head."

I proceeded to wash the wound with saline and then used a syringe to bathe the cut with Novocain before injecting the numbing liquid directly into the gaping slash. After suturing and bandaging him, I went to the doctor to get his signature for the prescription I wrote authorizing a tetanus shot and painkillers. The doctor was passed out on a couch in his office. I signed the damn thing myself.

Clift got off the procedure table. "I got some buddies I want to call to come and pick me up. Can I use a phone?"

"Of course," I said.

When his friends arrived, he shook my hand as he left.

"We okay?" he said. I looked at him with a dead stare. "You and me, we're okay, right?" he repeated.

I dropped my head for a moment to think how I felt. I looked up. "Yeah, we're okay. I'm a corpsman and this is what I do. You're a Marine. Now you know what I do. So yeah, we're cool."

FMSS training went quickly. Don, KC, and half my corps school class finished with me. We were proud and also nervous. Nonetheless, the accomplishment left us psyched up.

One thing bugged me, though. I had not found guys I could be myself with. We were so busy I never picked up on other gays though

I'm positive they were there. One thing's for sure, I never wanted to shove away another gay man like I'd done in boot camp. I wanted to find a pal to stand with me against Asshole Cliff and his ilk. For now, though, I was alone.

As dual-service sailors, we received the green-machine uniforms that we would wear while assigned directly to the Marines. As I put on the heavy dark green wool class A for the first time, I changed. I became that tiny bit narcissistic that men have to be in order to project confidence and strength. I began to think of myself as a man, a desirable man. I practiced my smile to best catch the light in my teeth and hopefully snare someone's interest. I had begged the heavens to make me an adult when I was young. Now I felt it. The avocado green trousers were the ultimate big boy pants, and I liked them.

I had successfully kept my secret from Don and KC. We'd been together since boot camp. We hung out together a lot and went drinking on liberty often. The seal on this friendship was the orders that we received after we finished FMSS training. Most of the other corpsmen were assigned to Marine units set to go in-country Vietnam. Our orders were different. We were assigned to the USS Repose (AH 16), a hospital ship known as an auxiliary hospital in Navy lingo. We had won the lottery by getting a plum assignment aboard a ship that would be stationed off the coast of Vietnam, as did about fourteen other guys we were in Corps School with. But upon reading our orders more closely, a caveat stopped our celebration. Our official assignment was to 1st Battalion 9th Marines.

"Hey, look here." Don pointed to a paragraph on my copy of our orders. "We'll be switching from ship to shore duty when needed. We're going to be a team of corpsmen that will be mobile."

I read the paragraph. He was right. "Looks like we'll be going between duty in-country and duty aboard the Repose," I said.

"What do you guys think?" KC asked as we blinked at each other.

"We have a fifty-fifty chance more than our buddies of not going directly into combat," I said.

CHAPTER SIX

Nam, Here I Come

After training, our orders were to report to Travis Air Force Base for transport to Vietnam. Since the base was seventy-five miles east of San Francisco, we headed there for leave before going overseas.

Don, KC and I flew up. Don's father had moved to the West Coast by this time and offered us a place to stay before shipping out. He even loaned us a car.

"Let's do the town up big," KC gushed. "I say we get drunk like sailors on leave. Might as well maintain that good name given to us Navy guys. A buddy of mine told me about a freak show that we have got to see in Frisco."

I had never been to San Francisco and really did not know anyone from there, but the term "Frisco" always grated on me a little. "So what is this freak show you want us to go to?" I asked, already suspicious of what he thought of as "freak."

"It's called Finocchio's, and listen to this, they have men dressed like women doing song and dance routines. It's supposed to be so weird because some of the guys look like real women." KC chortled on about queers, freaks, and men in dresses.

I got that same sick feeling that I had when Cliff was harassing me in FMS training.

"I'll call us a cab," Don said. "I don't want either of you two drunks driving tonight."

"Well, speak for yourself," I replied.

The taxi drove us to the North Beach area of San Francisco. It was seedy with a multitude of strip joints dotting the boulevards. Bright red and yellow neon signs reflected off every window, creating a garish glow. Half-naked women stood in doorways enticing sailors and Marines on liberty. The military had declared the area off limits because thugs would roll a drunken military guy.

The cab pulled up to a tacky building painted black. Above the door read a sign "Finocchio's, America's Most Unusual Nightclub." We entered.

It was a creepy show that reminded me of a Doris Day or Dinah Shore music special on television. The drag queens lip-synced to those singers' songs and affected a fifties period look.

I was appalled by the show's rank portrayal of gay men. The representation was that gay men were freaks who really wanted to be women. The joint was full of judging patrons only too willing to believe that the drag queens represented every homosexual in the world.

That night, I drank to get drunk.

I did not explore the real delights available in San Francisco to a man like myself. The city had already made itself the Mecca of my underworld. But I was with my shipmates and had no time to be gay. The beauty of the city on the bay captivated my imagination, however, and I promised myself that someday I would live in San Francisco. It was an open city with a growing gay subculture.

I also realized my shipmates would never be my confidants. I could never show my true self to Don and KC. I got a whiff of danger from their actions and talk that night and I suddenly feared them.

The day to ship out came too quickly. Don's father drove us to Travis. We didn't talk much on the drive. A new Beach Boys song came on the radio as we entered the base, "Good Vibrations." I loved the song, but I wasn't feeling the good vibrations that it promised. I was apprehensive. The song would forever remind me of that day in the fall of 1966 that I left for war. Even today, I pause when I hear the song. No matter what I'm doing or even if I'm speaking to someone, I go quiet for a few beats. The flicker of a movie starts behind my eyes, and a few quick images of what happened in that year play.

We gathered in the EM Club waiting for departure time. I was worried about the war, but my larger fear was controlling my gay urges and being discovered. So I drank. And drank. My inebriation was such that my friends carried me to the aircraft and I was almost denied boarding by the flight officer. If I didn't make that departure, I would have been technically AWOL. My friends promised to be responsible for me and begged him to let them take me aboard. I awoke over the Pacific with the worst hangover in history at thirty-five thousand feet. It was a shitty way to go to war.

We skipped across the Pacific, stopping first in Hawaii to fuel up, then on to Wake Island for more gas. The island designation is really a misnomer. It's a sandbar with a U.S. military airbase located about halfway between Hawaii and the Philippines. The appropriately named Midway Island, famed for the World War II battle, is north of Wake and used as a refueling stop for military flights, too.

Since it was fall stateside, we'd dressed in Navy blues, heavy wool. The humidity felt like a wall as I deplaned during the layover at Wake Island. The damp pressure on my chest made it nearly impossible to breathe. But we had no chance to change into our lighter, cooler, dress whites or Marine utilities. We were told that when we reached the Philippines, we would lay over for a few days, meaning we had to wait until then to change uniforms. The crew chief told us it would be even more humid in the PI, as we called it. I didn't understand how that could be. It was ninety-nine percent humidity at Wake Island.

Our plane was a behemoth C141 Starlifter. It had only two windows and was filled with motor vehicles and men, all going to war. Rumors ran wild, especially one that we would get a break and see some real high-style entertainment when we arrived.

"Diana Ross will be singing at the EM Club at Clark in Angeles City, PI," said one of the flight crew.

I didn't believe it, but even on the rare chance it was true, I was too hung over to give a damn.

We landed early in the afternoon and were disappointed to find we'd missed Miss Ross. We had the date wrong because we'd crossed the International Date Line, putting us a day ahead. We were also on daylight savings time, so in essence we had no idea of the fucking day or time when we arrived. All we knew was it was hellishly hot, hellishly humid, and we'd missed out on Diana Ross.

Green military buses arrived to take us to the Navy base at Subic Bay. We were told we'd be assigned quarters in transit barracks.

Subic Bay Naval Base had been in and out of U.S. hands for a couple hundred years. The port was used by all ships operating off the coast of Vietnam for resupply and repair work. Vessels ranging from the aircraft carrier USS *Enterprise* to the smallest frigates and everything in between made port-o-call here.

The ride took us from the airbase at Angeles City to Olongapo City, which was situated on the shores of the protective bay that made it ideal for a Navy port. It was late afternoon, and we passed through the city and into the countryside quickly. The roads were bumpy but passable through what I guessed to be towns. They were made up of poorly constructed buildings of cinderblocks and open shops with no windows or walls onto the street. The scenes reminded me of Tijuana in Mexico, which borders California. The people, like those in TJ, were very poor. I wondered what they dreamed about. What the movies in their minds were like. As a child, I knew we were poor. I hated it, and I wished to someday get away and create my own life. I doubt any of these poor people could even dream to get away. Instinctively, I knew they had zero opportunity.

It became too dark to see much. The roads became winding and rutted so badly that no one slept. The jungle canopy made the night darker. With nothing to light our way, we sat jostling around in our seats looking out windows into black nothingness.

KC, Don, and I managed to hold our clique together so I had company. It was 0100 when we arrived at Subic. We showered and changed into Marine utilities, which finally liberated us from our by-now musky wools.

"Hey you guys," KC said the next day, his voice brimming with enthusiasm. "There's a Quonset hut down the way that the locals have set up to make American-style breakfast. Some guy told me we should go there and skip the chow hall. They have Denver omelets."

When KC was excited, his voice rose to a squeak like Barney Fife from "The Andy Griffith Show," making Don and I laugh as we hurried to the hut.

"What's in a Denver omelet?" I asked.

Being from New York City, Don was the most sophisticated of our threesome. He was a solid handsome man, from good Italian stock. He was twenty-one and legal, which made him the "man" of our group. His maturity had helped when we studied together in Corps School.

He laughed. "Great, you're as ignorant as Alabama Boy here, sheesh. Well, my young friend, imagine three fluffy eggs wrapped around fresh-picked mushrooms, bell peppers, a bit of onion, and fancy sliced ham to make it sing like your mama. I suggest you go for it, Lara."

I loved the way he talked. It was so Brooklyn it made me want to watch an East Side Kids movie.

I followed his advice. The crunch of the bell pepper surprised me, and the Filipina waitress suggested a little jack cheese to go in it. The flavors melted in my mouth. I'd eaten only chow hall food for so long that heaven was right there in the Quonset Hut.

We stayed two days, finally getting notification we were to fly out of Subic Bay aboard a DC3, a small plane carrying soldiers to the front. It was right out of a 1930s black and white movie, like the plane in "Shangri-La."

The crew chief had been correct, the humidity was worse in the Philippines than on Wake Island. But when the flight officer of our DC3 heard me bitching, he said, "Just wait. You ain't seen nothing yet."

Evidently, there existed a place with humidity beyond a hundred percent. The joke had gone on too long. I was miserable in the humid heat. I was glad I'd not received field duty with a Marine unit. I couldn't imagine the hell men experienced humping through a jungle.

We flew into Vietnam, landing at Da Nang airbase. It was October and raining like the devil, which was typical for the time of year. The Southeast Asian rainy season starts in October and continues into January. From the air, Da Nang airfield was surrounded by buildings and shacks made of brick red mud with funky tin roofs. The rain made the air oddly cool. The promised humidity would wait to rear its ugly little wet head later.

We disembarked to the holding area. The storm was coming down in sheets, soaking us within seconds. Don tapped KC on the shoulder and KC signaled me. They were checking out a bunch of poncho-clad Marines standing under a lean-to near the helipads.

"Looks like something out of 'Sergeant York'," I mumbled. I remembered the movie for its frequent scenes of Army dudes standing in the rain waiting for war. But in this country, the movie changed to a sepia tone—red mud and grey rain—where the Marines' drab green ponchos made all color wash out of my view. Instead, I saw things in bronze shades of dark and light, giving me a picture of living in the opening segment of "The Wizard of Oz." It pretty much stayed that way while I was in-country.

A Marine officer met us in the waiting area.

"I'm 2nd Lt. Turner, and I'll escort you men to your ship." We were a group of twenty, many of whom I had trained with, who had orders to the USS *Repose*.

"Right now we have no place for you to stay so we're moving you into some unfinished buildings until I can contact the *Repose*. These will be transit barracks if they ever finish 'em."

We boarded a military bus and drove a short distance from the airbase and settled in one of the unfinished buildings. There was no furniture so we sat on piles of collapsed cardboard boxes.

"Permission to smoke, Sir?" Don asked.

Our escort nodded and we sat smoking while LT went out to talk with the busdriver and returned with an update. "Just sent a message with the transport guy to find out where your ship is. She's heading to headquarters at White Elephant Landing. We should hear back in a few hours."

We moaned in a chorus. He laughed and lit a cigarette.

Then we heard a whomping sound. Our escort narrowed his eyes. "That's incoming. Prepare to move!" he shouted.

Suddenly 107mm or 140mm tube-launched rockets rained on our position, falling only fifty yards from us. There was a row of six structures that would someday be barracks. Our group ran from one side entrance of a barrack to the next. With every move, the rockets followed us like the ones in those stupid Roadrunner cartoons. Boom! Boom! We raced through four structures before the shelling stopped.

As things finally quieted, we looked expectantly to LT. "That's it," 2nd Lt. Turner said. "I'm going over to White Elephant Landing and getting you guys some cover. Wait here."

He ran out and stopped a truck to check where it was going. He looked back at us children looking out of the barracks windows, nodded and off he went. We sat waiting for the next shell to drop.

Welcome to Vietnam. I'd only been here one day. We heard gunshots off somewhere, nothing really near. We were all green and worry marred every man's face as we sat puffing on cigarettes.

Turner finally returned. "I got a ship you're going to spend the night on. There's a mike boat waiting at White Elephant. It'll take you out for the night. They're having trouble finding your ship, or they were having trouble. It's back at Subic Bay so as soon as they can evacuate us from here, most of the group will fly back to the Philippines to meet her."

Two half-track vehicles soon pulled up, and we piled in. Like the tourist that I was, that we all were at this point, I stared at the scene of fighting that we'd just gone through. A small band of Viet Cong had attempted a raid on the Da Nang airfield we'd just come from. For the first time, I saw our enemy, dead on the ground. Mutilated bodies from multiple, and I mean multiple, gunshot wounds from our defending Marines. The bodies were all akimbo, their arms and legs lying at strange angles. I looked away; I didn't need to see anymore since I figured more was coming anyway. I later learned that when a man dies in a hail of bullets, his body position always end up in an unnatural pose.

As we rode to the landing, LT came up to Don, KC and myself. "Because you men have dual service status, you three are going to stay in-country and TAD someplace. I'll see you tomorrow morning after chow with your assignment. You will join the *Repose* once it returns to 'Nam."

The rain poured down for the entire drive. We got to the landing and jumped into the waiting mike boat. "You'll be spending the night on an attack personnel transport ship called the USS *Cavalier*," Lt Turner said. "I'll stick with you guys until we can sort you out."

The *Cavalier* was anchored in the middle of Da Nang Harbor, close to Monkey Mountain, a large, conical peak like a volcano. I would become very familiar with Monkey Mountain because of multiple trips back to this bay. It was like a big green giant squatting over the landscape. Besides our band of corpsmen, there were Marines also looking for their units here on Dante's ship.

The personnel hold of the ship was right out of Dante's inferno. The racks were stacked seven high. To get to the top, you used each rack like a rung on a ladder. Fun stuff if you're in the middle and the top guy gets up in the night to piss. We numbered two hundred guys in this "hell hold." There were three of these spaces aboard that transport. On top of the close quarters was the constant rolling of the ship. At least I was dry; I had a chance to change my clothes to fresh fatigues. I found a bottom rack, hoping that was a good choice for getting some shuteye.

Besides our band of corpsmen, the hold housed a bunch of Marines looking for their units.

"So this is the shit. 'Nobody knows where nobody goes' is what we've learned," said a young Marine I slept under. "Hey, you got any smokes?" he asked me.

I handed him one.

"I been looking for my unit for three fucking days now," he said, "and from what I hear that's SOP here in the Nam." He continued bitching until we had to hit the sack.

After a night aboard the transport ship, another mike boat took us to a pier near the airfield. Our brother corpsmen went off to board flights to Subic Bay to join the *Repose*.

Don, KC and I stood waiting for our assignment. "They're sending you guys up to Dong Ha, which is where the real fighting is," LT said.

"Boys, are we in for it now," KC said as we prepared to board a Huey heading up to Chu Lai, the first leg of our trip to Dong Ha. "There's shooting and bombing every minute, rockets I think."

I didn't know how he got this information. I hoped it was scuttlebutt because that sure as hell didn't sound like fun. The battalion up there carried the charming name of "The Walking Dead" because of the sustained fighting.

"Mucho casualties up there," said one of the chopper pilots when we boarded. He'd noted our corpsman insignia and felt compelled to share this so we knew what to expect.

We hopped and skipped north from Da Nang, first hitting Phu Bai then Chu Lai, where we boarded a Chinook chopper for a much longer haul on the final leg of our journey.

It was late at night when we arrived. Our copter had two headlights mounted on the front undercarriage, illuminating the airfield landing area. It was made of metal plates that had regular sets of holes in rows on every plate, like a cheese grater. There were hundreds of them.

The Chinook set down among about ten other choppers of various sizes. Rifle shots and mortars erupted around us as we landed, but they posed no immediate danger. The shells landed three hundred yards off and the gunfire was distant.

Although it was after midnight, a cook brought chow trays for the three of us with just a barbecued steak sitting on each.

"Sorry for the limited menu," he said. "We're short of rations, and besides, it's late."

The meat was tough but had a smoked flavor that my hungry stomach interpreted as good. Don, KC and I didn't speak. The wringer we'd been pulled through and the lack of coordination affected us into silence, or maybe it was the shooting we heard in the distance.

We sat at a wooden picnic table of makeshift construction. Someone's a carpenter, I thought. Above me a single naked twenty-watt bulb hung from a wire. The light made the room darker somehow.

I could hear a generator pounding away. The switch for the light was a metal bead cord. From the end of that hung a long greenish-yellow tape coming out of a Marine-machine-green colored tube. Stuck to the gooey tape were a million black flies. As I ate, I looked up periodically to make sure the number of flies on the tape hadn't decreased.

The head corpsman entered while we ate. "Awright, you guys. We got racks for you down the way. Horn and Zielonski will be back from a dust-off soon, and they'll get you settled in. You'll bunk with them until your ship comes in."

"How long you think we'll be here?" I asked.

"Just got word that the *Repose* is here on station, just down at Chu Lai. She'll be there for a little over a week. The guys you were with were rerouted over to her tonight. So I figure maybe ten days or so. Meanwhile, we got work for you here."

Just as we finished eating, a couple of corpsmen walked in, their jungle fatigues wet with sweat. The promised jungle humidity was all around us now. The night air held microscopic droplets of water on its hot breath. I hated how my skin felt and decided I was sleeping naked for the rest of my tour.

The corpsmen had a wild look to their eyes. Adrenaline does that, I soon learned.

"Hey, you guys. Lara, Johnson, and Amadeo?" asked a cute, blond, short fucker. The other one, Zielonski, was a goofy-looking, stocky guy.

"Yeah," we said in unison.

"Grab your shit and come with us." the blond said. At that point, I would have followed him anywhere.

We trailed him and Goofy down a row of Quonset huts, formed of green canvas stretched over metal half hoops attached to wooden platforms that served as floors. He stopped at one and told us this would be our billet. The hut's floor was dry and held eight racks with lots of room for us to stretch out. No one seemed to be up for sleeping so we grilled Horn and Zielonski about the situation.

"This is it. You're sleeping in the battalion aid station area," said Horn, the blond. "We have beaucoup guys with malaria just down the way from us. Believe me, malaria is far better than other shit you'll be seeing."

I understood what he was getting at. Malaria, while a serious illness, was easily treatable and rarely fatal. Not so much with battlefield injuries. "How are conditions where you were just at?" I asked.

Disgust marred Horn's face. "We're winning the losing battle." He must have seen the confused look on my face so he continued in a more serious voice. "Casualties are light for now. I figure you guys will work in the surgery area." It was obvious he was being sarcastic at first, but truthful. I liked him.

"What're your names?" KC asked.

"I'm Joe, he's Matt," Goofy said. "I been here three weeks so I'm just as green as you guys. Horn here is a salt, been here, what? Three months, Horn?"

Matt answered in the affirmative. As he, KC, and Don talked, I couldn't help but notice that Matt seemed real nice. I mean in that way ... nice. Even Joe was giving me homo vibes and I wondered if the impossible had happened—had I just found a tribe to hang with?

It was late. I headed to my bunk. I stripped to my T-shirt and skivvies and fell into my rack. But there was no letup in the humidity, and despite being dead on my feet with fatigue, I couldn't knock off. Finally, I stripped naked and it didn't take long to fall asleep.

The next day the three of us were assigned operating-room orderly duty. We split shifts between us; I drew the 2000 to 0400 watch, which meant I could catch shuteye on a stretcher in the OR if no business came in. Sweet, I thought.

Things were quiet. My first duties as a real corpsman were to learn how to wrap steel surgical tools in a special paper that could withstand the heat and bit of steam the machine produced to sterilize them in the autoclave, which looked like a tiny iron lung. This was the best technology we had at the time, and it was effective. But it gave off a peculiar smell that I didn't like. I got in the routine of cleaning and autoclaving surgical instruments over the next few days.

One night Matt pulled operating room tech duty the same time as me so I began to chat him up. Next thing I knew, I was giving him my life story.

"My dad used to beat me. He abandoned my mom and us kids just before I started high school."

"Why did he beat you?" Matt asked.

"I was a disappointment to him. I wasn't the kind of boy he thought I should be, I guess. I didn't like sports. He was an asshole who used to run around with other women. He even told me he'd gone to bed with just about every woman he ever knew. That disgusted me. I think it showed on my face because he accused me of only making girls my friends. He said that's not how a man should act. I wasn't looking for girlfriends anyway."

I hoped that was enough to give Matt a hint of where I was coming from. I was fishing because either it was wishful thinking on my part, or this little fucker, who was hot as hell, was giving me the gay look.

I was probably deluding myself. He was masculine and tough, hard like a Marine. I couldn't imagine having the luck of finding guys like me my first turn in Vietnam so I swung the conversation to him.

"So how about you. Where you from?"

"Born in Fort Scott, Kansas, then I lived in Springboro, Ohio, for my high school years. I was raised Roman Catholic. Didn't go to Catholic school, but religion was very big at home. You know, reciting the rosary while kneeling in the living room once a week. We had to say prayers on our way to school before we could listen to the radio. My sister and I did them as fast as possible. If we were lucky, we'd get one full song in before getting dropped off." His laugh was restrained and fun to watch. Choking a bit from laughing at his own joke, he asked, "Were you religious?"

"Mom was Jewish, dad Catholic, but they left it up to us kids what to believe. I never chose so I'm nothing."

"You said you never had girlfriends. Why's that?" Matt asked, with a slight grin.

The code words for being gay had already been invented, such as "Friends of Dorothy." But those signals had not reached Vietnam yet.

"Let's just say, it's not a priority right now," I hedged.

"Me, too," Matt said, then paused for a time before continuing. "I was about seven when I started having crushes on my teachers. I had a gym teacher, Mr. Bagley. Every time I saw him in a jockstrap, I had to run away." He peered into my eyes. He had no grin and showed no fear. He was one bad motherfucker, and he'd just gone balls-out with me.

"I was about five when I realized I was different." I told him the story of the blond Mexican field worker I'd noticed at an early age.

"So you like blonds?" he asked as he looked at the hair on his arms. He was all blond.

The conversation was getting uncomfortably close. I switched subjects. "And Joe?" I asked.

"Bingo! Him, too."

We shared a laugh as our duty ended, and we ambled back to our tent for some shuteye, not making a big deal of what just went down, but inside I was happy. I'd found my tribe, my buddies. I was sorry I'd be going to the *Repose* soon but I'd be back because my orders said so. Plus this was going to be a long war. I learned that in my first few days in-country.

———◆———

The base had not had any fighting since that first night so no casualties were coming in. Word was getting around that a big operation was underway. The military top brass named coordinated pushes, and this one had the name of Hastings Two. The goal was to deforest the tops of a bunch of hills in the area then setup perimeters around those tops to allow us to shoot down on the enemy. The hills were designated with numbers, Hill 884, the object of Hastings Two, being one of them. But for now nothing was going down so I had an easy time.

In war, things change quickly.

After six days, word came that the *Repose* would be heading up to us so Don, KC, and I would be sent aboard as soon as it arrived.

"Hey, Lara. Matt and I want to give you a little going away party. Come on over to the supply tent after your watch." Zielonski was all smiles. We'd not been able to speak about our shared secret again. This would be our last chance until I returned.

When I finished duty, I strolled over to the supply area and entered the storage tent assigned to the OR. Zielonski and Matt sat on wood crates drinking something out of the tin cups we were issued for drinking.

"What's in the cup?" I asked.

"Hooch, honey," Matt said. "Good old fashioned whisky hooch. A rare thing in a war zone, but Ski here was able to procure some off a supply sergeant who has a thing for Polacks." Matt was feeling frisky. They had already knocked off a couple of shots.

I sat and joined them.

"I'm from Philly, Germantown to be exact," Ski said when I asked him about himself. "I'm the only child of immigrant Polish parents. I joined the Navy to get out of the tiny house we live in and to breathe air that is not smothering. I'm Catholic like Horn, and while he is all positive about being gay, I'm still having problems. For now, life is too short to worry about it. I have my sergeant to keep me company, and so I drift along trying to stay alive like the rest of the jarheads."

"And working? How's it been here at Dong Ha?" I asked.

"Loving men makes me care about all of them. I know you're going to see it sometime, but dust-offs are the bitch." Dust-offs were medical emergency chopper pickups. "I'm not so much scared I might die. I'm more scared that I might lose a man during evac."

We talked for two hours about war and men, doing shots of hooch with nothing but more shots to wash them down. Then Ski's sergeant stuck his head in to say goodnight. Ski gave me a cute wink as he left with his sergeant. Matt and I policed the area to get rid of our cigarette butts and the empty whiskey bottle. We were drunk, but still standing and only slightly stumbling. When we finished clearing up, Matt preceded me out. As he reached the door, he turned to me.

"Can I kiss you?"

He didn't say it in a shy way, but he was respectful and moved toward me only after I nodded. Our mouths met first, just lips. Then our tongues touched. We held each other tight and kissed long and hard. I was attracted to Matt and obviously he was attracted to me, too. We broke off the kiss, but he continued to hold me tight as if he wanted to protect me. It was like he was saying he had my six when things got tough. There was no time to do anything more and without saying a word, we both decided not to get ourselves worked up for nothing. We were sleepy and went to our respective racks.

The next night we got word that the *Repose* was due off our coast in the morning. I was pulling duty in the OR, which was a huge tent in Ringling Brothers style, divided into four areas with three operating rooms. I worked in the fourth quarter where all the surgery tools were cleaned and sterilized. All the supplies were held there, and my job was running supplies to the operating teams. My section of this huge tent opened to a small courtyard, like a sundeck off a house, but instead of a wall around the courtyard, sandbags were piled five feet high. It served as a smoking area, eating area, and a place to get air for the men that worked surgery.

At about 2300 hours, rockets rained down, targeting the chopper landing area near the airfield. I lay on a stretcher looking out at the open end to the courtyard, and I could see our flares soaring into the air with a whoosh, and then a sudden burst of bright blue-white light that bathed an area about the size of a football field beneath it. Half a dozen of these things hung above a long section of the wire. Just above the brightness, a tiny white parachute slowed the descent of the flare. The Marines were launching phosphorus flares to illuminate the area outside the wire in the hopes of seeing Charlie approaching our perimeter, but I only saw shadows that jumped and danced in the underbrush surrounding our camp. The flares frightened me as their light seemed ineffective.

Suddenly, there was an explosion in one of the malaria tents not far from my billet. I held my breath. My job was in the OR tent, so running to the explosion was not an option, but I was desperately thinking of the injured. I didn't hear the telltale siren of an incoming rocket. I'd already heard that sound close-up while in Da Nang. Confusion filled my head as to what had happened.

"Hey, get up! We got wounded!" Matt yelled. He'd pulled back a tent section leading to the operating room right next to me.

"What's the haps?"

"Sapper got under the wire, spreading charges around the camp," he said in a rush as he left. I'd already learned that VC commandos, called sappers, would sneak onto our bases and plant explosives.

"Holy shit!" I sputtered.

I started gathering the equipment I knew our surgeons would need. I could hear Marines moving in my area obviously looking for the sapper. It was dark, street lights didn't exist in a war zone, but then I saw a dark figure dressed in black pajamas slip into my courtyard. He was trying to hide in the shadow of the sandbags. For a moment I looked at where I thought his eyes were, trying to gauge when he would lob the grenade and calculating the kill zone of an exploding Soviet model. Then, in a burst, a couple of Marines who'd been on his tail each fired a barrage that cut the guy off at his knees. He crumpled. They rushed in and disarmed him, grabbing a small bag of explosives off him.

I walked into the courtyard, stunned. The two Marines looked down at the guy and then at me.

"You all right?" one asked.

I nodded. The guy was still alive; the surprise of it took my breath away.

"He ain't no good to us for intel. Look at him. Bet you a carton of cigs that he's dead in ten minutes," said a Marine.

"Twenty. This bastard's a tough little asshole. I say he'll live longer," the other replied.

They weren't laughing or being mean. It was just a curious reality to them, one they seemed comfortable with. Men died here. It was the way this man was dying that made them curious and in a betting mood. I stood thinking, wait aren't you going to finish the job? But they walked off and left him.

"We'll check with you later, Doc," one said.

I stood for a second, staring at the black pajama guy lying on the ground as I heard wounded being brought into the OR behind me. A Marine was screaming.

All corpsmen acquired a tactical knife the moment we got in-country, a KA-BAR with a seven-inch blade. We kept it on our utility belt for easy access. It was meant to cut away difficult webbing and anything that needed to be cut in a hurry. I fingered the leather-covered handle lightly without really thinking as I looked at the half-alive man. He was barely moving. I took out my knife and studied the small thin man for a moment. I'd learned during the autopsy class in Corps School where to insert it. I plunged my knife just below his sternum, angling it up toward his heart. He died instantly.

I returned to the tent to prepare the things the surgeons would need. I worked the entire night alongside Matt.

I never saw again the Marines that made the bet, nor did I ever tell anyone about what I'd done. I only knew that the screams of the wounded Marines were ringing in my brain and perhaps made me want to get revenge. Maybe I even felt sorry for the pathetic bastard. All I knew was that it was them or us.

As the dark turned into morning, Matt and I walked back to our tent tired from the long night. We promised to keep in touch and meet up as often as possible. A few hours later, I boarded a Chinook chopper with my sea bag and some of the wounded from the explosion.

———◆———

As we flew out, the USS *Repose* sailed into view, a white ship sitting atop a blue ocean. It gleamed in the bright sunlight of the morning, and I thought of white nurse's shoes. I remembered having to polish those shoes when I was a candy striper. The ship had that same chalky white coloring. From the height we were flying, it looked tiny, like a pearl on water.

"We're going to land on that?" Don asked a chopper crew guy.

The makeshift helipad had been added to the fantail of the old converted Liberty ship that now was a floating hospital. The pad looked miniscule. We landed with only a few feet on all sides of the chopper to the water below.

As I disembarked I handed my orders to the flight officer. He handed me a pamphlet that had a pencil drawing of the *Repose* and above it in script print was the title: "The Angel of the Orient." The chopper revved up to lift off, and the officer shouted into my ear.

"Welcome aboard, sailor! We call her 'The Albino Bitch'!" He pointed to the fancy title on the pamphlet then directed me toward a waiting corpsman to start my orientation.

I'd been in Vietnam twelve days. It seemed like a month already. Time had begun to slow down. I worried that a month would seem like two, that two months would seem like six and that six months would turn into years. My orders were for thirteen months. I was eighteen-years-old and it seemed like forever already.

CHAPTER SEVEN

USS Repose AH-16

The USS *Repose* comprised a complement of seventy officers and four hundred and ninety-eight enlisted. Half were the ship's crew. The other half was hospital staff; approximately thirty medical officers, both doctors and nurses, and two hundred and fifty enlisted men of various medical designations, most being hospital corpsman.

She was configured with an eight hundred patient capacity, but generally we ran about five hundred patients. This information came from the "History of the USS *Repose*" section of the pamphlet handed to me when I arrived aboard.

The floating hospital operated mainly in the "Eye" Corps area of Vietnam, which included Da Nang, Chu Lai, Phu Bai, Dong Ha, and Quang Tri, including the DMZ. In 1954 the United Nations established the demilitarized zone by splitting Vietnam in half. This line set the border between North, the Communist half, and the South, the democratic half. Since the United States did not acknowledge the legitimacy of North Vietnam, we would say that we were stationed in the northern part of Vietnam. The DMZ saw some of the war's most intense battles. (After treating more than nine thousand battle casualties and admitting more than twenty-five thousand patients for inpatient care in Southeast Asian waters, the *Repose* would depart Vietnam on March 14, 1970 for the United States.)

I had a few days to become familiar with the ship before getting my assignment.

"Anyone here that's been on the ship awhile?" I asked when I got to the corpsman compartment. Only about six men sat around, I guessed the others were on duty. No one answered, so I grabbed KC and we investigated all the areas we could access.

The corpsmen compartment was just above the water line. I could tell because when I opened a fire hose cap leading to the outside of the ship, the ocean was about twelve feet below. All the enlisted crew's quarters were at this level or one below. These lower levels also held the chow hall, galley, laundry, storage, water distillation, engine rooms and surgery and morgue.

One level above corpsman country was a mixed-use area with several different departments. Going aft, a metal plate sign showed petty officer quarters. The "geedunk" store and the post office were in the mid-ship area. Down the central hallway, we passed the dental clinic, optometrist, and administrative offices, plus three of the ship's hospital wards.

KC and I stopped at the geedunk store to get some ice cream and chat with the store clerk.

"What does geedunk mean anyway?" KC asked.

"No one knows really. The way I heard it was that it is a bastardization of some Chinese word meaning lazy. Some writer during World War II heard sailors say it when they talked about getting candy and sodas from a ship's store onboard a troop transport crossing the Atlantic. He used the word in his story and it's been in use ever since."

Each deck above that level contained mostly hospital wards and officers' country, with the last top interior deck being A-level. Here were two general medical wards, the officers' ward and the nurses' quarters. The officers' ward had a nice galley that prepared food for them.

The exterior decks started above the corpsmen quarters level. All these decks were made of wood. Most of the lifeboats hung on A-deck, each suspended above a wide esplanade of fine teak planks. This gave the Albino Bitch the air of a cruise ship.

At the ship's crown, a large, tarp-covered space was where crew and patients could lounge shielded from the intense sun of the South

China Sea. Some superstructures and smoke stacks dotted this top area. While exploring the upper levels, a passing deckhand heard me refer to the "wheelhouse." He stopped to explain.

"It's called the bridge, sailor. How the hell long you been in the Navy?"

I still had a lot to learn.

"Hey Lara, KC! Where you been, buddies? We've been wondering where you went off to," came the shouts when KC and I descended into the corpsmen quarters after our journey around the ship.

"We've been exploring," I answered.

Some of the men we'd been separated from in Da Nang were now in our bunk area shooting the shit. Salty talk emanated from the group with scattered calls of "I ain't see you turds since the Philippines."

"You mean for the last week and a half?" I said.

KC wandered off, leaving me to give them the lowdown on our run through Vietnam.

On board were about twelve guys I went to Corps School with, and even a few that I'd been with since boot camp, including Don and KC. So my original military family was there and that made the transition to shipboard life real easy.

About two hundred and fifty corpsmen were bedded down in our quarters, but our jobs and watch duty had us going in and out all the time. I didn't get a sense of it being crowded. It was cramped but comfortable. The nurses were all female officers, and a rarity, but the corpsmen were all male. Enlisted women didn't pull sea duty, but due to the nature of the *Repose*'s mission, we had women onboard.

The racks in my sleeping area were only four high. I was glad for that fact after the night on the troop transport with its seven-tier rack configuration. It would have been tough duty if I had had to live in those conditions for my entire time aboard. Three ladders descended into our dimly lit space. The showers, sinks and a couple of urinals were on the starboard side. Toilets, more urinals, and a few sinks were on the port side.

I found a top rack on the starboard side, right at the aisle that led to the showers. I had a full twenty-five inch clearance above my head. The normal distance on anyone in the lower bunks was about eighteen inches between the bunk above and the one below it so I had a pretty good spot.

Thankfully, the area had air conditioning, and I had my own personal duct next to my bunk. However, at the times we needed air conditioning the most, it was rationed. The machinery was not able to handle the tropical humidity for the entire ship, and the wards and OR had priority. When we lost air conditioning, it was like living underwater, hot water.

The lockers in our area were located around the bulkheads of the sleep compartment. A narrow, three-foot aisle circled the bulkhead with the lockers facing outward relative to the ship's interior and into the narrow aisle.

I grabbed an open locker in the bank located on my side of the ship. Each locker was perfectly sized to hold the contents of a sailor's regulation sea bag. There was a little extra space for personal items like books.

"Say, you can store a pint bottle of hooch in here too," KC drawled as we unpacked our stuff into our locker.

Since finding Matt and Ski at Dong Ha, I realized there had to be more of my kind in this man's Navy. So I began to scope out my crewmates for other "sisters." It wasn't difficult. I spotted Dave Monarch upon arrival on the *Repose*.

As I came down the gangway from the chopper, there he was, one of the very few black corpsmen I'd seen since joining up. He looked cool because he had a gold tooth next to his front teeth. With his ultra-dark complexion, he stood out, especially with the gold tooth. But there was one thing in particular that screamed gay. He had his bellbottoms pegged. This was a sailors' tailoring trick to make their pants fit tight at the hips and crotch, with a tuck at the knee that made the bell flare pronounced. It wasn't so unusual, but he even had his work dungaree blue bellbottoms pegged. Who did that to work uniforms? And the area around his crotch was tailored so tight you could practically count the veins on his cock shaft. His basket, the bulge in his pants, was the biggest I'd ever seen. He was a nice guy, but projected an aggressive sexual energy. In other words, he had a dangerous black guy vibe. Was I being racist? Probably. Despite the sensitivity training I had in high school, I was still a product of my time. I thought of myself as liberal, but I felt uneasy around him and sensed danger. I decided not to hang around with him.

I continued looking for a tribe of guys I could be real with. While I respected and even loved those twelve buddies I'd been in school or boot camp with, I needed to find gays. It was like a hunger, a need to find men who shared what frightened me.

After a few nights I began to meet the men in my bunk area. They were a super nice bunch of guys that I quickly learned were fun-loving and eager. On the third morning after arriving, my eyes opened to a man staring at me. Across from me, in the row of racks that mirrored my side, was my second gay sighting.

"I'm Bobby, but everyone calls me Sponder," he said impishly, lacing his fingers together to rest his chin on while lying on his stomach.

He was in the second bunk from the top, directly across from me so we would greet each other every morning and night. His comment made me laugh because we called each other by our last names, so he was being cute.

Bobby was a spunky little blond, about five-eight with a soft body that would probably become fat as he aged. We went to chow together. He was funny as hell, and we took to each other immediately. We didn't ID each other as gay at first because that just wasn't done back then, but we both knew. Our humor and the movies we liked (he loved "The Sound of Music") pretty much sealed in each of our minds what we were about.

"Where are you from?" I asked.

"You mean my last duty or where was I born?" He knew what I was asking but he liked to joke around. If he was asked a question, he would answer with a question. I was thinking he was going to start every conversation this way.

He decided to answer his first question first. "After Corps School, I was at Boston Naval Hospital for a while. Then a buddy and I heard about the *Repose* and put in for a transfer. We wanted to make a difference. I was tired of plain ward work. Really these wards are the same as stateside, but this means being closer to the action. I guess it's because I hope I can save a man's life."

Corpsmen took on a serious mantle when we talked about our job. We all had that something in us that Bobby voiced. That duty to save lives was ingrained in every man and woman who became a corpsman, from the moment we finished our most basic training in medicine. It was working in combat conditions that completed us. Made us what we were meant to be.

"But to answer your real question," he said with a twinkle, "I'm from Columbus, Ohio. I live there with my aunt right across the street from Ohio State University."

I thought of Matt. "I seem to be meeting a lot of guys from Ohio lately," I said.

Bobby laughed easily. "Yeah, Ohio is a good place to be from."

In short order, he introduced me to Tom Conkin, his friend from the Boston Naval Hospital. Tom had a thick Boston accent, stood about five eleven and had thick, curly, blond hair that always looked as if it needed a haircut. He never would achieve that regulation Navy hairline.

"So I see you've joined our little group of brothers," Tom said, looking at me with a conspiratorial grin. He was hunched over and slightly turned, like the witch that held the apple in "Snow White." I started laughing out of relief as I realized I would have these two impish, funny, intelligent, and gay, guys with me through whatever was in store. "I'm a recovery room tech," Tom said. "I have my rack in a special billet down in the hold where the OR is. That's why you don't see me up here much with you guys. Come on down to post-op sometime and you can help out."

Maybe the war wasn't going to be so bad after all. I immediately began to plan on how to get the five of us, Matt, Ski, Bobby, Tom and me, all together.

———◆———

"Lara is it?" asked HM2 Brinks, a big black corpsman that I reported to for my first assignment. "My tour is up next month. You'll be taking over for me as ward nutrition corpsman. Basically, it's chow duty for A-deck patients who can't leave their beds, wards one and two. These guys are mostly general medical patients; migraines, malaria, minor concussions, parasites, and so on. Combat injuries are on different wards, depending on the injury. Those are contained in the decks below us here on A-deck."

"You mean I have to serve the bedridden patients like a steward?"

"First, you cook the meals, then you serve. You got a problem with that?"

Damn right I had a problem, at least at first. How the hell was being a glorified cook using all that Corps School training? I wondered if Brinks had done something wrong to get this duty since he was an E-5. That was a high rank to me, an E-3.

But it turns out that my medical training was not wasted. I still had flight quarters duty, which utilized all of my medical training.

"Flight quarters, flight quarters," the PA system boomed when wounded were incoming. Choppers, both Hueys and Chinooks, brought patients directly from the battlefield.

It seemed that this call always went out at 0300. Flight quarters were jarring enough during waking hours. To be roused out of bed at three in the morning was disturbing, and often traumatic, depending on how bad the wounded were.

"Conkin, I have flight quarters duty today. What am I expected to do?" I asked before my first shift.

"I'll join you topside on your first shift. Just come on down and grab my ass. The ropes, as they say, will be shown," he replied.

My first call came in at O-dark-thirty for ten ambulatory and twenty-five litter patients. We carried and walked them into a holding area where medical teams waited to evaluate each soldier.

"This process is called triaging. We're going to get the casualties, both stretcher and ambulatory, off choppers and bring them into the triage area. Things happen quick here. First you're going to help by stripping off their clothing and do some fast cleanup on them. They're going to be dirty and bloody. Use scissors if you have to."

Tom had situated me at the bottom of the ramp so that I could watch my first incoming patients before getting into the fray. I was a young, inexperienced corpsman. He wanted to be sure I saw the process from beginning to end. He'd joined the group removing men from incoming choppers and as he passed me, I followed him into the triage area.

"You're going to hear screams and some of these men will be really torn up. So get a grip and just move. You're going to find that you will know exactly what's needed just by the training and duty you've already had," he said.

It was a busy night with a lot of badly wounded Marines. The men were coming from Chu Lai, a support airbase and jumpoff for operations just south of Dong Ha. It was located off the beach backing onto the sea. The Viet Cong used this to their advantage by lobbing mortars and rockets on the base from the jungle to the east. The casualties came in with shrapnel wounds to every body part. Legs looked like they'd been cut with saws, jagged and bleeding profusely. Some torsos were pockmarked by flying hot metal, which caused round dark red-blackish holes. Then there were the head wounds; sometimes missing parts of the skull. The triage area filled with teams of nurses and doctors handling each man.

"Doctor, this bandage is filthy. I'm sure the bleeding has stopped. Do you want me to change it?" I spoke quickly as I stripped the uniform off an unconscious guy with a head wound. The doctor looked over from a gurney on the other side of my man.

"Cut it away and put a compress bandage loosely tied. I'll look at it in a second."

Activity swirled around me frenetically but it was orchestrated and efficient. Twenty people worked in a small space of about 350 square feet. Everyone was speaking and pointing at once. I got snatches of conversation. Shorthand, clipped phrases that everyone understood.

"Clamp,"

"O blood stat."

"Corpsman! Move this patient to pre-op immediately."

There was no time to get into the details or question the orders. Do it, keep moving, I told myself. Move! Move! Move!

So even though I was cooking and serving three meals to about twenty patients during the day, on my off-duty hours I used my medical training working in triage—setting up IVs, cutting away clothing, handing medical instruments to doctors and nurses.

"Triage. Where did that word come from?" I asked the chaplain as he came up next to me while I worked on the head wound. He was a fixture with incoming patients.

"It's a French word that was probably coined during their Revolution," he answered. "The meaning was established in a time when there were no medical options and yet those poor people tried their best with little knowledge and supplies. The word is used to determine the severity and chances of living for the wounded. It's an emotionally cold process and has relevance to us here."

He became pensive and sadness crept into his voice. "Because you see, in war, when you identify a patient that the doctor deems unlikely to live, he goes to the end of the line. His chances aren't good anyway so no intervention for now. If time and people permit, then those who've been moved to the end will be worked on. We have limited resources, so only those that have a chance get treated first."

The chaplain was morally struggling with the cold, yet logical treatment of human life. I stopped asking questions like that.

From triage the patient either went directly to the OR or to a bed in a ward that handled the patient's injury or wound. Not every guy coming off the field needed surgery right away. The wounded were prioritized with the urgently wounded but survivable going directly from flight quarters to be operated on, while others went to wards to get cleaned up and would go under the knife later.

Wards were organized by the patient's medical condition. We had urology, orthopedics, and intensive care units. Other injuries were sent after surgery to another specialized ward specifically for post-op patients. There was also my general medicine section.

Tom soon realized that I knew what I was doing when it came to surgical instruments. So as things became controlled on my first flight quarters, he asked me to join him below in the operating room.

"I need your help in pre-op and post-op. Now my job starts as the surgery team moves into motion on the guys needing immediate attention."

I followed him, stripping off the medical gloves I was wearing. "I can get those instruments for you." I said as we got working. "I know how to setup suture trays. You go on and do what you have to do. I promise I won't get in the way."

Tom smiled. "Thanks. You're going to be a real help, and you have a good attitude."

So I got to use my corpsman skills despite being a glorified steward. This was my first real duty station, and now I was part of a hospital staff doing what I was trained for.

We'd been on patrol off the coast of Vietnam for about two weeks when word came over that we would head to our main port of supply, Subic Bay. I'd already spent time there and was looking forward to having a Denver omelet again at the Quonset hut restaurant.

The cruise took two days. Once we hit port, a miraculous thing happened with my patients who were unable to get out of bed for meals. They got out of bed just fine. Any patient who was well enough got liberty, too.

Brinks winked at me as he said goodbye on his last day aboard after making port. "Now you see why an HM2 like me has a job like this. It's plum when you get to port. Take care and good luck." He knew what I was thinking about him and the job we did on A deck.

Being a glorified steward meant there was nothing to do while in port. I knew I had landed the best duty ever. It was pretty much the same thing for Tom because all the operations were done by the time we docked. Bobby worked in the urology ward, but even his workload lightened a bit. It was the badly wounded wards where the guys still had a regular duty schedule. The orthopedic, ICU and surgery units were busy all the time.

There was a town just outside the main gate called Olongapo City that I had not visited on my last stay. The town owed its existence to the harbor and by extension, the American presence, which meant that Olongapo City was a bustling boomtown due to the war. Australian, British, and the odd Canadian ship also made port at Subic. Olongapo was jumping and thankful for it.

A California crewman, a chunky cutie nicknamed Bubbles, schooled us corpsmen about Olongapo as we sat on A deck. We had just entered the bay and were moving into position to dock.

"If you've ever been to Tijuana, Mexico, think more. More bars, more honky-tonk music bands, more prostitutes, more debauchery than saintly TJ could ever possibly muster," Bubbles said.

The prostitutes meant nothing to me. But booze and bands, what was not to like?

"Anything can be bought here in Olongapo for very little money," Bubbles continued. "So what are you desperate for?"

"Me? I want a steak," I said. "I've not had a piece of meat since my first night in Dong Ha. Steak seems to be in short supply here on the

Repose. So for our first night out I think Tom, Bobby, and me need to find us a superior steak dinner."

"You gotta get yourself on a jitney, then ask the guy in your best pidgin to go to Papagayos. There you'll find a T-bone steak for sale that beats them all in the entire Pacific. Trust me on this one," Bubbles said.

Our gaggle walked across the bridge leading off the base and into town. The city consisted of two main drags in the shape of a T. The main one and the longest, Magsaysay Drive (pronounced Magseesay), ran up to the base gate. A small bridge crossed a particularly odious river that separated the city from the base. Bubbles had charmingly called this waterway "Shit River."

We quickly found a jitney, which were taxi-like vehicles that only cost twenty cents. They were actually miniature gas-powered flat-bed trucks with benches in the rear that passengers jumped into for rides anywhere they wanted to go. As we jumped in, Tom sat looking at the city before us.

"This looks like the perfect spot for a missionary," he said as we took off into the bright lights and madness that was Olongapo at night.

Everything was cheap for a sailor on leave. A pack of cigarettes was only twenty cents, so life was good in Olongapo City. But beyond the flashing lights of bars and restaurants on the main drags, poverty existed on a scale that 1960s Mexico would have been ashamed of.

To our surprise, because you can never trust the ship's crew for good info, we got to a really nice restaurant that indeed had the finest steak in the entire Pacific. Many of the ship's officers and crew were there as well, and we enjoyed a great dinner our first night out on liberty.

KC had joined us and chatted up one of the nurses next to our table, talking about the dinner we had finished.

"Really, you can't get a bad meal here in Olongapo," she said. "Sometimes you might be eating dog or monkey if you buy off a street cart, but go to a reputable restaurant you get pretty much what you want and at a good price."

To get the lay of the town we walked back to base along Magsaysay. Every other doorway was a bar, and every bar had the best cover band you would ever hear anywhere in the world. The Filipinos are masters of mimicry; the big song making the rounds was "Black is Black" by Los Bravos. We had already heard it four times coming out of bar doorways as we walked by. I remembered hearing a sailor onboard talking about something called the "Olongapo National Anthem."

"Hey guys, I just figured it out! 'Black Is Black' is Olongapo's national anthem." Bobby, Tom and KC laughed at the truth of my statement.

We bopped in and out of bars on our way back, settling on one called Club Oro.

"Hey guys, I'm going to take off and head back to the ship. See you later," KC said.

That left Tom, Bobby, and myself. Tom was the first to break the ice. "Okay boys, now that we're finally alone, I have to ask: Marines or sailors?"

I stared at him trying to understand what the hell he was asking. He and Bobby broke into laughter like two high school girls at my confused face.

I blinked for a moment and finally got it. "Both! But if I was to tell you the truth, any man will do. I'm so glad to find out I'm not the only lavender boy on the Albino Bitch."

"Oh boy, another one," Bobby squealed. "We'd been on the ship for three weeks wondering when we would find more sisters for us to dance with. When Tom saw you, he was sure. But you know the Navy. It's too dangerous to just assume. Tom, you are so bold asking that question."

"I maybe mince my walk at times, but not my words, honey. I knew David was one of us, so I thought I'd just ask. To you two." He lifted his glass. "A toast to found friends. Thank god we can now let our hair down."

We clinked our rum and cokes in celebration. Just then the bar girls began circling us like sharks. We already knew that the girls were not all prostitutes. But whether they were hostesses or prostitutes, they expected to be paid for their company at a table. Usually the bar had a one-for-one policy in which sailors bought a beer or cocktail, and the hostess sitting with you got a mystery drink. I call it "mystery drink" because it was a very diluted whisky and whatever soda the girl liked, and no surprise, it carried a premium price. Olangapo's economy was set up to separate a sailor from his money and what better way than to offer dollar beers and girls who ordered two-dollar mystery drinks and demanded tips.

"The girls are beginning to surround us. What the hell are we going to do?" a panicked Bobby asked.

I decided to take charge and beckoned one of the girls.

"Can I speak to mamasan?" The pretty Filipina nodded and went to get an older, but still attractive, woman who was in charge of the stable of women. She came over all smiles and bent down when I indicated I wanted to say something private.

"Look-see, Mamasan. We not interested in girls." I winked. "Understand?"

Totally unfazed, she nodded and touched her nose with a finger. Then she scanned the room. In a corner, she caught the eyes of three bar girls talking together. As they sashayed over toward us, we looked to each other baffled by this response. The three extra pretty girls pulled over chairs and sat next to us ready for their drinks to be ordered.

"No, no, Mamasan, no girls. We don't want girls," I pleaded.

"You bakla, yes? You only like boys, yes?" I looked at her helpless with both my hands in the air, palms up, as I weakly nodded.

"These ladyboys for you. You like them. Be nice and buy drink for ladyboys," she said with a toothy grin. Then one of the girls took Tom's hand and placed it under her mini skirt.

Tom shrieked with delight. "The ladies are boys! Come on man, that's it. We have the company of transvestites tonight."

We bought drinks all around. The ladyboys were entertaining and fun. I wondered what the other military men thought but soon realized they were clueless. Our table looked, by all appearances, like every other table in the joint. My ladyboy was beautiful. Her name was Vangie, and I asked her if we could be friends.

"Yes, sailor boy. You come to Club Oro, and I make sure no girl bother you. I be your friend all time," she said.

I knew I now had the best cover. Anytime we sailed to the Philippines, I could look respectable at Club Oro with my lady friend.

We stumbled out drunk as hell and looked around for a ride back to base.

The next day I described our crazy night to Bubbles, who chuckled. "You got called 'bakla'? That means nancy boys. She pegged you. By the way, I'm bakla too." He winked.

It felt good that I had my gang to be with, even a deckhand, too. The laughs and fun never ended while there. But five days of liberty didn't last long. We headed back on station off the coast of Vietnam way too soon. When we got back off Dong Ha, the ship newspaper announced that the *Repose* would spend Christmas underway to our next port-of-call, Hong Kong, for six days of R&R.

This became my first opportunity to bring together the two groups of guys that would share this journey with me. I sent a quick letter to Matt letting him know of the *Repose's* plans to spend the few days before New Year's in Hong Kong. I knew he and Joe would make it. I had learned that Matt was good at getting what he wanted. Wangling a few days of liberty was a piece of cake for a combat corpsman like him. Plus I wanted to follow up on that kiss he gave me my last night in Dong Ha.

I looked forward to 1967, but I knew that five weeks on station in Nam were going to be long. I was always looking for diversions.

———— ◆ ————

I was working my main duty doing chow runs for guys too sick to get down below and standing night duty for flight quarters. Bobby worked the urology ward, and I would visit him when I had time off. One day I sat talking to him on the ward.

"You can only stay a little bit. The Pineapple Princess will be back soon and kick you out." He had begun calling the head nurse on his ward, Lt. Wong, the "Pineapple Princess" because she was from Hawaii but the princess part really meant "bitch" because of her squared away attitude.

Suddenly, a Marine in a bed nearby shouted, "Corpsman up!"

Bobby jumped up, grabbing an unmarked silver spray can and ran to the patient. All I saw was a flutter of white sheets and yells coming from both him and the patient. The Keystone Cops had nothing on Bobby when he got going.

"What the fuck?" I said as he returned with a smile on his face.

"That's Zeke. He had lace curtains when he came to the Nam and was not the most hygienic in that area. He's onboard for a circumcision to fix the little head so no infections will pop up in the future…ha. I said 'pop up.' He's a randy fucker and gets the ol' boner fairly often, especially in the morning. This here can," he held it up, "is full of Freon. I run over when he yells for a corpsman and spray that tally whacker off with this cold stuff."

"Why all the comedy?" I asked, mouth agape.

Bobby chuckled. "That's just me adding a little drama. The boy laughs so much that it won't stay hard very long. I mean, when was an erection a laughing matter?"

The mischief in his eyes danced in a delightful way. I was laughing so hard that when the Pineapple Princess came in and gave me a look of disapproval, I almost peed my pants as I was propelled out the door.

A few weeks later the *Repose* set sail for R&R in Hong Kong.

CHAPTER EIGHT

The Group

It took two days of sailing to arrive in Hong Kong. As we headed north, the weather turned cold. Suddenly, it was winter. We were ordered to wear full dress blues while in port. I liked that prospect. I was going to try being a real adult while in Hong Kong. I had plans of finding my signature drink, like a Gin Ricky or a Manhattan, something that sounded like a drink Rick would order in "Casablanca."

I was anxious to get my pants pegged like David Monarch's so I asked him for his tailor's name.

"It's on the Kowloon side. The tailor is W. W. Tang. Just use his name when you get in a cab, and they'll know where to go."

My average pay was a hundred and forty dollars per month. Add forty dollars in combat pay, and I was pretty well off for a young man with no bills. I sometimes sent my sister my combat pay. Her husband had left her and she needed help. Even so, I was rolling in the green stuff. Drinks and cigarettes were cheap. That only left restaurants and gambling. I stayed away from gambling, so cash was no issue.

Matt alerted me by mail that he and Joe would rent a suite for all of us at the Hong Kong Hilton and to report to the Dragon Boat Bar on the top floor the moment we arrived. They would know when the ship anchored. Sailors always knew secret ship movements.

I brought my two groups together for the first time in real style. The Dragon Boat Bar was possibly the most adult venue on the planet and what could be more adult than three sailors in dress blues and two combat Navy men in Marine Corps green dress uniform?

As my *Repose* group approached Matt and Joe, I had already instructed them on how we'd greet them, "Blue water detachment reporting as ordered, sir!" We presented a snappy salute and stood at rigid attention.

"Ah, fuck off," Matt said. "Sit down and have a drink then it's chow time." He said this while pointing to the very conspicuous boat in the shape of a dragon sitting in the middle of the room. A sumptuous buffet was arranged within it.

He and Joe had selected a table beside windows that went from floor to ceiling. The cities of Hong Kong and Kowloon glittered like Manhattan before our feet.

"Hey Matt, do you think we can forget the war for the next few days?" I said when we sat down. While the ship was on station in Vietnam, we'd been active, but casualties had been light during my first three months at war. The horror of war hadn't filled me up yet.

He snickered. "I'm ready to leave it behind me right now." His eyes clouded over as if he was looking at something.

Joe, too, dropped the smile on his mouth. "It'll be there when we return. So for us, we joke and drink and eat too much for tomorrow we may die."

"I see sarcasm and a grasp of reality is still intact," I said, while thanking my lucky stars that I'd met men who knew truth and did not delude themselves. This fucking war had already changed me. I was more intelligent about life, but also more cynical.

As we partied, I decided that scotch and soda was my drink. Sailors on ship said that in Hong Kong, real scotch drinkers mix it with milk. I never tried that but it sounded much the same as Christmas eggnog with brandy.

"Awright," Matt announced after we had eaten and drunk our fill, "time to repair to our quarters. We'll have to double up on the two beds and someone will need to sleep on the couch. But it's fancy and roomy. You're going to love it."

We took the elevator down two floors. When the suite door opened, I yelled, "Bitchin!" It was Western-style but had an Asian ambiance with paper room-separator doors dividing the space between a sleeping area and a sitting area. Two king-size beds took up most of the sleeping area. The sitting room was spacious and had black leather couches and red and black lacquer tables and chairs.

A gay band of brothers was forming, and we all just wanted to stay in and talk. We sat around the living area and ordered liquor and snacks via room service. I didn't think any of us had ever done that before. "You know what this reminds me of?" I took off my jumper and shoes and parked myself on the floor, wearing only my bellbottoms and white t-shirt.

Bobby said. "'The Group'."

A howl went up in the room.

"You mean the Vassar movie about a group of girls during the thirties?" Joe asked.

Bobby nodded. We screeched in unison like a bunch of girls because we realized that we had now established what we as a gang were going to call ourselves. That coming together into a community was earth-shattering for 1960s America, let alone for gay sailors on liberty in Hong Kong.

Matt had not heard of the novel or seen the movie so Joe explained. "'The Group' is a novel by Mary McCarthy. The story is set in the 1930s, when eight young female friends graduate from Vassar College. It starts with their graduation and ends years later when one of them dies and they meet again at her funeral. It's all about how fucked up the world is to these women. They're expected to play a woman's role and cater to their husband's wishes. The movie is so good. You have to see it someday."

"But their overriding issue involves the men in their lives: fathers, employers, lovers, or husbands," I added.

We didn't know it, but we were subconsciously trying to find some kind of community to build for ourselves as gay men. It was the perfect setup for a bunch of gay men trying to figure out what kind of model they would use to map their lives.

"Let's pick names from the movie for ourselves. I'm Kay because she was the richest," Bobby said.

"And the fattest and laziest," Tom added. Howls went up and we were off to the races.

The bitchy queen had already entered the zeitgeist of the gay underworld. It was part of our DNA. I'd never even heard the word "camp" before but what we were doing was "camping it up" and it felt right. Were you born this way? asked the straight world, who thought they had all the fucking answers. To me it was obvious that I was gay from the beginning of my life.

Tom and Bobby were comfortable with what we as a group were doing. But I could see that Matt and Joe were having a come-to-Jesus moment, like I was. As gays, we felt disconnected from the world at-large but we wanted to be part of a world, too. I realized we had to make our own world, one in which I could be gay and not hate myself. It was just as natural for them as it was for me to start camping it up.

Tom quickly took the name "Lakey." He began affecting the Garbo-like tone à la "I vant to be alone."

"Contrary to what Kay just said, I'm the wealthiest in this group," he said in that Garbo way, winking. "I'm the dark beauty, with pale skin, black hair, and large green eyes." He fluttered his eyelashes like a silent screen vamp.

Lakey's story line has her living in Europe for most of the novel, where she earns a doctorate in art history. At the end of the book, she flees the war in Europe and returns to America. The Group assembles at the pier to greet her and finds her accompanied by a baroness, her lesbian lover.

Tom dropped the Garbo affect. "I've not found my baroness yet, but I'm sure as hell going to try."

Laughter and general rolling around on the floor ensued. Names were passed around, and I became "Polly."

"When you think about my life, it is sort of like Polly's. Her family suffers financial losses due to the Depression. My family was dirt poor. She is pretty, well that's me to a T," I said, to general laughter. "And she worked as a technician in a local hospital."

"Well, there you are," Matt said, as he rested his hand on my shoulder. "That's pretty much you."

I gave a sidelong glance. "You, Matt, are Helena cause she's a short, sandy-haired girl with an appealing snub nose. Her humor is really quite droll, which is *you* to a T, and her mother has her tutored in every conceivable subject, including athletics, musical instruments, outdoors activities, and crafts. So even though she's a graduate of Vassar, she gets a job as an instructor at an experimental school in Cleveland teaching finger-painting."

"Hey," protested Matt, "just 'cause I'm from Ohio? Besides, I can do more with my fingers than painting." He danced his eyebrows up and down like Groucho Marx, causing all of us to bust up laughing.

I finally called lights out as the clock hit 0200. "We've got big plans for mañana," I said.

Tom and Bobby took one of the beds, and Joe and Matt took the other, but Matt stayed talking with me in the sitting area for a while.

"How did you come to this gay thing?" I said. I was desperate to hear how others had navigated to this point in their lives.

"I guess I first realized I was gay by getting a crush on a male teacher in fifth grade. I didn't think about using the word 'gay' until I went to college and started having crushes on all the guys. Until then, I just really thought it would remain a secret forever. I dropped out of college after a year and decided a change was necessary. The Navy seemed a good alternative. I actually thought I would keep my secret here, too. But after meeting Joe and now you, I'm quite happy being gay."

"I know what you mean," I said. "I actually thought I hated sex and was so ashamed of myself. But now that I have grown a bit, I'm okay with it but I still have conflicts."

Matt thought for a second. "You mean because we can never have a relationship, and I don't mean marriage. I know that's impossible. But a committed relationship with someone you love?" He paused before continuing. "Right now, it's all about tricks and lovers. Ha! You'd think we were prostitutes the way we've adopted those terms, and the only thing gay guys are about is the sex." He stared at me. "You know what I want, David?"

I didn't answer.

"I want to find someone to travel through life with. I wish, I wish."

"I know." I was saddened. I'd never thought about what being gay meant in the long run, that we could not have marriages or even life partners, like straight people could. For the first time, it dawned on me that being gay could mean a lifetime of loneliness.

I was still sitting on the floor. Matt reached down and pulled me up onto the couch and wrapped his arms around me, as if protecting me from the feelings I was having. We talked more.

He was twenty and had a decent family life. He had one sister. His parents had adopted a Chinese girl when he was young. It was nice to hear that having a father that beat you didn't create a gay man. That was a perverse thought I had been harboring. But here Matt was describing the perfect TV family, and he's gay.

"My parents were cool, but they're ignorant about my truth," he said. "I really thought I was damaged somehow. But talking with you has made me realize that we weren't created by outside forces like society claims. We just exist. That must mean we're okay."

"I could talk with you all night, but we gotta go to bed," I said.

As we stood he put his arms around me and kissed me again like he did that night in Dong Ha. His tongue entered my mouth, and he touched and flicked mine as we kissed. I wanted him but he pulled away and smiled sadly as if to say we had no privacy. I lay on the couch and as I waited for sleep, I thought of that kiss and what it might mean.

There was mounting dissatisfaction over British colonial rule in Hong Kong. There had even been riots on the Kowloon side, which was Communist-controlled. Living and working conditions were appalling, and corruption in officialdom was prevalent.

The main part of the city comprised densely-packed high-rise buildings and rickety apartment buildings pushed up to the foot of a large mountain range. This density caused the creation of a huge water city called Aberdeen Village, where peasants lived on floating boats called sea-going junks. We'd been kibbitzing over breakfast that morning about what to do that day, and some of them talked about taking a tour.

"I feel it's disrespectful to gawk at those people and their condition," Matt said. "Can we do something else?"

But Tom had already appointed himself tour director. "As a matter of fact I've already hired a tour car—like the jitneys of Olongapo—to take us to the Tiger Balm Gardens. They have amazing vegetation, but the real attractions are these strange plaster and cement sculptures." He flipped out a dog-eared pamphlet. "According to my guide book, we will find oddly shaped thingies everywhere in the park."

We went to the Tiger Balm Gardens. As we walked into the park, we encountered the first of many bizarre and wonderful structures, a crudely carved horse head splashed with blue paint in no particular pattern, and on top of the horse head was a pagoda-type temple with tiered roofs. The building had those pointy little outcroppings that you'd see in any cheesy Chinatown architecture back home.

Up to this point I thought those buildings were just American fortune cookie ideas of Asian buildings. But these temples and sculptures were beautiful, and I was happy to learn Chinese immigrants brought this design with them when they emigrated.

The designer of the gardens was a man who became rich when he created Tiger Balm, an ointment used for skin ailments. It burned though, as Joe learned when he applied it to his lips. "Shit, my eyes are burning, too!" he yelled, jumping up and down like a spoiled child.

"There's camphor oil and menthol in it, you ninny," Tom said with a laugh. "Don't put it on your mouth and don't touch your asshole either if you want to avoid a shock."

I was thoroughly entertained by every one of the men in my group. We spent the day walking the gardens of Tiger Balm forgetting reality.

The navies of the world were congregated in Hong Kong because of the American war in Vietnam. The city made a perfect liberty port for ships deployed in the conflict. Men needed time off and this city offered R&R in abundance. Free-drink coupon books were offered to us everywhere we went. Two-for-one specials or a free meal were offered to entice you to buy more liquor, the real moneymaker.

Matt came up with the idea to have dinner that night on Victoria Bay. "I got two rickshaws outside. Let's head down to the bay and hire a water taxi to take us out to the Tai Pak floating restaurant."

Bobby had been making a fuss about the restaurant since we'd arrived because he remembered it from the movie "Love Is a Many Splendored Thing" so he was all for going.

"I found some information at the concierge desk. We can have what is called sumptuous Chinese fare, most of it being the innards of strange animals, but who cares. I'm going to try some steamed fish intestines and barbecued duck feet. I found something for you, David—snake soup. You like long slender things."

We were still laughing as we boarded our rickshaws for the fifteen-minute ride to the water's edge. We got into a water taxi and as it floated from the shore I said, "I suspect we will run into a bunch of our shipmates. So get ready to butch it up and not get us kicked out of the Navy on our first big night out."

The Group gave me a knowing nod. Matt sat next to me during the ride. "I have lots of experience in hiding who I am. High school was fun. I had a bunch of good friends. So I felt no pressure to be sexual with girls because I could use the excuse that I didn't feel ready for that, and since I'm Catholic, it was a perfectly acceptable answer."

"You didn't feel lonely?" I said.

"No. Well, I did feel lonely with myself, but like I said I had a lot of really good friends. My friend Danny got to use his parents' car on the weekends and we'd all pile in and go to this park. The Cuyahoga River runs right through it. We had picnics and went on hayrides. The river was full of shale, and we would hunt for fossils and go exploring in the woods. We never drank or took any kind of drug. Nobody even smoked. We were the most wholesome group of American kids you could ever imagine. It was ideal."

"But it didn't last?" I prompted.

"It changed the moment I graduated from high school. I could feel it as I was leaving the graduation ceremony. Everyone was moving on and nobody wanted to go on hayrides anymore. Girls started thinking something was wrong with them when I didn't want to have sex with them. Then they started thinking there was something wrong with me." He shook his head. "That's when I felt isolated, when I became an adult."

Our taxi pulled up next to the floating palace that was Tai Pak Restaurant, and we dropped our conversation. His openness flattered and charmed me. I was beginning to really like Matt.

We bobbed our way off the water taxi onto the most amazing boat. The Tai Pak was a huge floating lantern of red and gold lights and two decks of divine decadence about half the size of a football field.

As The Group walked in, we saw other shipmates and we collectively turned off our gay selves, fading in with the world as it was.

"Hey hey hey!" KC yelled from across the room, "Matt, Joe! How the hell did you end up here?"

I had not told KC, or Don, that I was in communication with Matt and Joe. As gay men, we needed to keep our friendships private. Too much information about our circle might put us all in jeopardy should one of us get discovered. The military had interrogators specially trained on questioning homosexuals and getting them to inform on others.

"I decided to give them a heads up about our liberty in Hong Kong on the off chance they could come," I quickly answered.

"Come join our table. There's a bunch of us from the *Repose*." KC wrapped his arm around Matt and escorted us to a long table with a dozen of the corpsmen from our ship. As we sat, Matt gave me a sidelong glance when KC positioned himself between him and me.

We consumed enough alcohol that we dared one another to eat the frog and squid that was presented to us. I did and found that I liked squid. We soon became just that little bit sailor drunk, and KC seemed to be putting the move on Matt. I decided a break was needed.

"Matt, let's get a cigarette outside on the deck. We'll be right back, KC." I hustled Matt away from the table.

"Are you sure he's straight?" Matt said off the bat. "The fucker keeps putting his hand on my leg and stuff."

"I don't know much about these things, but I think it's because you look really handsome in your dress greens. You're super masculine." Matt's eyes smiled. "You know how guys kind of get almost gay-chummy on football teams? It's their testosterone kicking in and they bond like gladiators. It's sexual, but they just don't know it. They're scared as shit to do anything about those feelings. But here, it could mean trouble."

"That's what I was thinking. Alarms are going off in my head to run from this guy."

I finished my cigarette and we headed back in. Matt looked over his shoulder as I followed. "So you think I'm handsome, huh?" He licked his lips and flicked his eyebrows up.

When we returned to the table, KC and some of the other *Repose* men were squaring off with a bunch of British sailors. I smelled the start of a fight and shot Bobby a what's-up look

"KC was trying to make off with one of the Limey's hats, saying something stupid about Donald Duck losing his cover. I think chairs are going to start flying. You stay here with Matt. I'll round up Joe and Tom and let's dee-dee out of here," Bobby said.

He returned with our Group just as the fight got going. Boom! A chair flew on to the Brits' table. I didn't know who threw it, but the rumble was on. The Group jumped in to grab some of our shipmates and leave.

I spotted some British sailors pinning down Eslava, one of my boot camp buddies, and beating the daylights out of him. I turned to Bobby. "Let's make like Laurel and Hardy. You get down on all fours behind the Limeys. I'll distract them and shove them so they trip over you."

Bobby, his face serious, got into position as the British sailors were giving our friend kidney punches. I faced them head on. "Hey, you fuckin' wankers." As I had thought, they didn't like being called out for beating their meat. They stood and I pushed them over Bobby. They fell in a tangle of limbs.

Bobby jumped up and pulled Eslava to his feet. "Just like in the movies," he yelled, and bumrushed Eslava to the gangway. I'd spotted a convenient water taxi ready for a quick departure. All of The Group was in it, each having rescued other *Repose* corpsmen.

Matt and I sat in the back laughing our asses off when Bobby yelled, "Who paid for dinner?" The five of us looked at each other and a collective hoot went up. "Nice dinner for the price. Looks like none of us paid."

Matt and I looked back. KC and the rest of our crew were in another boat heading to shore. KC stared at us as our water taxi veered off to a different dock.

"At least they made it," Matt said. "I just hope KC doesn't cause us any trouble."

Our ride back to shore turned into debauchery as Bobby sang in full voice the theme song from the movie that inspired our dinner that night, except he changed the words:

"Love…is a long and slender thing
It's in Andy's nose…that only grows
into a long springy thing.
Love….is nature's way of giving
a reason to be living.
His golden crown that makes a man a king…"

Luckily, the other crewmembers onboard were too drunk to notice the gay overtones of Bobby's bawdy lyrics.

We jumped aboard waiting rickshaws back to the Hilton. Bobby, Matt and I shared one. When we pulled up, Matt jumped off while I struggled to help tipsy Bobby off the contraption. But the rickshaw coolie let go of his handles, and, boom, the damn thing tipped backward, dumping us on the pavement.

Tom, Joe and Matt laughed until tears ran from their eyes; and I joined them, flat on my back and laughing so hard I couldn't catch my breath. We'd had a notoriously good time.

The next day, New Year's Eve, we trekked up the highest mountain in Hong Kong, Victoria's Peak. From there we saw the gleaming white ship that would be our home for most of the coming year. We could even see the red crosses on the sides of the Albino Bitch. At that moment I felt really proud to be part of her.

Singing strains of "love is a long and slender thing" on the way down Victoria's Peak, we prepared for a bang-up New Year's Eve. We'd gone shopping that afternoon, and each of us purchased Zippo lighters. Joe suggested a twist on the usual engraving sailors got on the lighters.

"Let's all get 'The Group' put on these instead of our unit's name. This way we have something to hold the memories we're making. When this is all done, someday we can take these out and remember the good times."

"Hell, yeah," everyone responded.

We returned to the hotel to check out and ready ourselves for the big night before we were to ship out the next day. Tom, Bobby and I took our things back to the ship, while Matt and Joe left their stuff with the doorman at the Hilton.

A British commander had given *Repose* enlisted men a New Year's gift of a free meal and drinks at a banquet restaurant, a nice place made for such gatherings.

We were told we could bring a guest each, so I invited Matt and Bobby took Joe. "Free booze and chow, I'm in," Matt said.

The party took place in the bottom two floors of a three-story establishment. The bar and restaurant were on the bottom floor, while the second floor comprised a terrace overlooking the main floor. The third tier was closed.

Matt and I danced around one another as possibly going further than just being friends. As impossible as that idea was, we were young and threw caution away.

We snuck up to the closed third floor to make out. What wonderful kisses. Toby never kissed me except for that first time we made love, and the sailor in San Diego, while passionate, had no feeling to his kisses. This was the first time that I tasted the playful dance of French kissing with meaning, as well as passion and desire.

"If we get a chance, I really want to make love to you," I whispered into Matt's ear.

"Me, too," he answered.

We continued, oblivious to our surroundings. Our pent-up feelings took over, making us unconscious to the dangers our actions put us in. We spent too long in each other's arms and away from the rest of the guys. Suddenly, we heard, "What the fuck!" Our heads whipped around to see KC standing in the doorway with Don.

My mind raced with possible excuses. It was after midnight. Could I claim we were only celebrating the New Year with a platonic kiss?

But KC had obviously been looking for Matt and brought Don along for his hunt. When they found us, they'd watched long enough to know that it was more than a fraternal kiss. We stood and fled downstairs to the crowd.

I found Tom and Bobby and hustled them out before KC could catch up. The ship was weighing anchor early so it was time to get going anyway.

Matt slipped away, not out of cowardice but duty dictated he and Joe get to the British Naval base near Kowloon that would provide transportation to Da Nang that morning. Their departure time was in three hours.

Back onboard the *Repose,* I went into the head to wash up. I was drunk and hoped to hit my rack for two hours of sleep before morning muster. But KC and Don were waiting for me. KC proceeded to slap and punch me around in the shower area yelling, "*You're* not a fag, are you? Tell me you're not a queer, David."

I didn't know why he was doing this. Maybe he was a latent homosexual and the only way he could handle it was by bashing a homo as proof of his straightness. We'd already been through a lot. We'd seen combat together but now he was beating me up for being a fag. Don finally intervened and pulled KC off me.

I was scared. This could ruin me for life. I took the coward's way out and pretended that I was too drunk to remember what had happened.

"I don't know what the fuck you're talking about. I'm drunk. Leave me the fuck alone."

God, I hated myself. I ran out of the head, climbed into my rack and passed out.

I lied about my essence, but it was survival.

CHAPTER NINE

A Dark and Stormy Night

An ominous feeling came over the crew as the *Repose* set sail from Hong Kong. The waves rolled into high swells and clouds blanketed the sky as we steamed into the South China Sea. This jarring switch of weather spooked the whole crew.

I woke that morning with an enormous hangover, but I hadn't been so drunk that I didn't remember KC catching me making out with Matt and slapping me around. As I got up, I was suddenly ashamed of my nakedness in front of my shipmates as I showered as if I was violating their space by showing my gay self to them. I was also terrified of KC and Don. What would they say? Would they turn me in?

Don and KC had been drunk that night, too. I reluctantly made eye contact with them and received no recognition of anything amiss. I wasn't sure if they even remembered catching Matt and me kissing. Maybe they'd decided to give it a pass.

I had no work on my ward so I had free time to hang out with Tom in his bunk area. I told him what happened.

"They remember, you can bet your ass on that," he said. "When I was stationed in Boston, I saw this happen often. Why these straight fuckers want to beat us up is a mystery to me but it happens all the time around gay bars there. My advice? You have to do something nice for them. One thing I have learned about this being gay thing is that people eventually figure it out. So to inoculate yourself from being exposed, you have to be that much better than anyone else in your unit. You have to go out of your way to do a deed that will tell them not to turn you in."

I didn't worry about it too much at that point. I felt like something bad was coming and the rest of the crew felt the same thing. Everyone had that look in their eyes as we passed each other on deck. I asked my deck ape friend, Bubbles, what was up.

"The barometer is in freefall. Let me take you to see it on the main deck."

I followed him up to the bridge where he showed me a shiny brass enclosure attached to the bulkhead just below the captain's window. Inside it was a clock-like affair with measurements that I didn't understand.

"See that arm pointing to nine hundred and thirty? That should be above a thousand," he said, pointing to the needles. "If we get down to nine hundred millibars, we'll be in the middle of a hurricane."

I wondered if barometric pressure changes could have an effect on mood, especially out at sea. I was trying to figure out why I was so edgy.

"There's some bad weather out there somewhere," he said.

The murmurs I heard later from deckhands solidified what Bubbles had told me. Finally, the head nurse came around to the wards and gave us the lowdown. "There's a typhoon nearby. The captain will be announcing to batten down soon. He told us we're going to try and skirt its edge. It's heading northwest of the Paracel Islands. It seems to be heading on a course that will take it right into Charlie country, Hai Phong Harbor in North Vietnam."

As if on cue rough waves began to batter the ship. The cross swell worsened, washing water over the rolling decks. The captain would not turn the ship into the swell because that would take us off course. He was trying to hold steady toward Da Nang while hoping to avoid the worst of the storm. The storm so far had been without wind, just high waves, but an hour later doors and hatches were banging all over the ship as the calm air erupted into pounding winds. An announcement came over the PA, "Batten down the hatches. Rig for heavy seas. Medical personnel report to duty stations."

On a normal Navy vessel this would have been done already, but I think our captain had been hoping for calmer water. Bubbles's boyfriend, Squawk, said the radio room wasn't getting accurate reporting about this storm.

We instinctively jumped to general quarters procedures. Traveling through the ship, men and women used the procedure of starboard-up and port-down when ascending and descending ladders between decks. Seriousness was etched on everyone's face as the crew and medical staff gathered at assigned watch stations.

I reported to my little kitchen on the A-deck wards, but the duty nurse grabbed me and took me to join the ward corpsmen, who had gathered for a quick meeting. We went into the treatment room in Ward A-1.

"All right, gentlemen," said the nurse on duty, Lt. Hildebrand, "We need to instruct the patients on how they can tie themselves down in their bunks during the storm. We also need to sweep the wards for rolling carts, loose chairs, anything that can roll off counters and shelves. Use duct tape where needed. I've never ridden out one of these things myself, but let me show you how we can use a sheet to rig a simple strap for the patients to use."

Our lesson didn't take long. Soon the corpsmen were demonstrating the procedure to patients. We had cleared the *Repose* of most of the wounded and sick before heading to Hong Kong. Anyone who could handle the move was sent to the Naval Hospital in Yokosuka, Japan, before we sailed for R&R. That helped a lot in prepping for the storm.

"Lara," the LT called as I talked with a couple of patients. She pulled me aside. "You're being reassigned. You'll be a ward corpsman from this day on for these two wards, and temp duty when needed in the officers' ward." The officer's ward consisted of about twelve private rooms in the A-level passageways heading to wards A-1 and A-2.

Now I get to do my real job, I thought. The job of chief cook and bottle washer had not been easy. I carried twenty-five pound round cylinders up five flights of ladders to bring the chow to my patients. Carting three of these fuckers three times a day was not fun, especially when the air conditioning was off in all but the wards. But now I had patients to care for, medically. I had become a real hospital corpsman.

The captain came on the ship's com-system. "We expect huge waves to hit us. A few have begun to break up to the bridge level. All hands are to remain below deck. Boatswains report for duty to implement rigging operations on lifeboats."

Looking out the ward window, I could see men heading out into the wind while waves as big as carriers came rolling at us. The captain pointed the ship into the waves. He was going off course, but it was necessary to prevent us from being sunk by a broadside hit from a mountain of sea. The sudden change could be felt. We'd been rolling side-to-side, but now the ship plunged into waves. The dips reverberated throughout the ship with each dive into the valley of a monster wave. The sky darkened to black.

After finishing battening down, I went down to corpsman country since I was off duty. I sat on the deck of our berth area with other corpsmen not on watch, KC and Don, a guy named Garcia, the Marine liaison Tony, and two other corpsmen not on duty. The floor was the most stable place to be. Anyone who crawled into their bunks soon found himself spilled into the aisles.

We were unable to see outside the ship in the bunk area. The few windows and portholes on other levels only provided a wet, foggy view of huge waves that could sink us. Every man was worried, corpsmen, crew, and patients. Soon our berth area grew claustrophobic. We'd all seen war movies where the men went down with the ship while water poured into the rack area.

"I feel like we're rats trapped in a steel box with water pounding all around us," I said to no one in particular. The looks on my pals' faces said they didn't like it there, either.

We could feel and hear waves sweeping the deck from stem to stern above us. "There are no patients in A-2 ward right now. We moved everyone into A-1 when we got underway to Hong Kong," I said. "Why don't we spend the night there? I'm not comfortable down here. Besides, we might be needed for whatever is coming topside."

Our scared little group voted unanimously to take my suggestion. KC grabbed my arm. "Thanks, David. I ain't shittin' you. I'm freaked out right now. I don't want to stay down here one minute longer. Really, thank you for coming up with this idea."

I had just inoculated myself. KC was beholden to me now and I was safe from exposure, just as Tom had instructed me to do. I couldn't help but feel a mission accomplished moment right then.

We made our way out, our bodies banging from bulkhead to bulkhead as we walked the halls. Navigating pitching ladders that were vertical one moment and horizontal the next made the trip to A deck nearly impossible. Up four decks to Ward A-2, we struggled with each step as the rungs shifted under every lift of our feet. Howling winds, pitching decks, and the occasional crashing noises told us that things were bad. Our only option was to keep a cool head. The band of boys I took to the empty ward settled in, using the sheet tie down method I had learned as we jumped into empty hospital racks.

"I'm hungry," I said. "Anyone want to join me on a run to the chow hall?" None were interested in dancing down five decks and then back up so I went alone. In reality, I found the trip almost fun, like a carnival ride back home. I was never again going to experience this kind of situation so I wanted to live every moment.

The chow hall was cold when I entered. No food could be prepared with the ship bouncing like a racing roller coaster. A couple of cooks stood watch and one answered my question about available food.

"The only thing to eat is horse-cock and cheese." He used the indelicate term we used for bologna. "Here's some bread so knock together some sandwiches. We also got some canned peaches, if you can handle sticky bits of peach landing on your utility uniform. Some potato chips, apples and oranges. That's it."

I grabbed what I could, putting sandwiches and fruit into an empty rice bag and returned to A-level. I left the canned peaches in heavy syrup.

As I handed out the booty, someone from a top rack leaned over. "Hey, what about me, fuckface?" It was Tom.

"Why are you here?" I said, laughing.

"My hole down below sea level is not a place I want to die, so I came up to join your little team. We're not exactly busy in OR."

"Nice thought," I replied. "Way to make us feel safe, dingbat."

With the wind and sea pounding all night long, I became seasick. Not even the saltiest of sailors could take this much pitch. Patients and crew alike stayed in our racks, but no one slept.

The typhoon broke early in the morning and an incredible calm took over. A beautiful sky greeted me as I stepped on deck, just outside my new duty station, the A-deck medical wards, for the first time in what seemed like days. I felt like a tourist on a cruise liner. After such a scary night the ocean seemed new and refreshed.

Bubbles walked by. "How dangerous was that storm in your experience?" I asked him.

"Pretty fucking scary. Our screws came out of the water once. Did you feel and hear that loud shudder around 0430?" I nodded. "The next wave was so big, it pushed the ship so that we were broadside to the swells. The next wave after that pitched us two to three degrees past rollover. I guess the ol' bitch can right herself, but the chance of us foundering was real. We weren't even in the real storm track. I don't want to go through another like that in this tub. It's just not made for it, and neither am I."

———◆———

Back on station, sailing up and down our section of the Vietnam coast, I settled into being a ward and flight quarters corpsman, happy that I was carrying out the duties I trained for. I could never say that this work was dull.

A lot of the guys arriving in my ward had malaria. When in-country and even on the ship, we were supposed to take a weekly anti-malaria pill. It was large, orange and gave you a day of diarrhea. I seldom took it. We also always had a handful of Marines with an infection that left them feverish and lethargic. We carried out blood cultures on the men, but were unable to identify the culprit. Viruses do not culture like bacteria, so perhaps it was something like that. I suspected the men may have drunk from streams with who knows what kind of pathogens. Later, stateside, I became a victim of this illness. It seemed it could lie dormant for years before manifesting. We also had cases of fungus, parasites and the ever-present flu.

On top of that, we had malingerers, Marines sick of war. I did not think of them as wrong or weak. I had seen only a fraction of what our troops went through in this war. I wasn't sure I could have been a corpsman who went on patrol like Matt and Ski, let alone a real foot soldier. Headaches were often the malingerers' complaint. Doctors always ordered spinal taps to test for meningitis, encephalitis and tuberculosis. Sadly, most were sent back to combat once the medical team determined them fit. On occasion, one would go crazy.

Each day melted into the next with a certain sameness: setting up trays of pills for the morning med call, assisting the neurologist with spinal taps, taking vital signs, or getting up at o-dark-thirty for triage in flight quarters. But it never became boring or routine.

Occasionally I got notes to Matt via a friendly chopper crewmember that often flew into the aid station at Dong Ha. Anytime we were on station near there, there was a lot of chitchat between Matt and me.

One day, while working with Tom in the recovery room, I was washing and sharpening 18-gauge needles, what I called the "big bores." These were used to deliver extra fluid into a man, such as when a guy was bleeding out. I would set up a bag of plasma with an eighteen-gauge needle so I could get the lifesaving liquid quickly into him. The smaller needles, twenty to twenty-six gauge, we used for inoculations and routine blood drawings. The eighteen-gauge needles were in short supply and replenishment was slow in Vietnam so we resorted to cleaning and sharpening used needles.

"We really need more of these bigger ones," Tom said holding an eighteen-gauge while speaking to the OR nurse. "Retreads are tough to insert, even sharpening doesn't really work. I was working a post-op patient yesterday and the needle would not penetrate his skin. It tore through like a shredder and caused a huge hematoma from the force I had to use to insert it into the vein. It was a nightmare, Lieutenant Commander."

Pain appeared in Tom's eyes when he described this. His empathy for the men he worked on was affecting him emotionally. "Besides, someone's going to get hepatitis if we mess up on this cleaning process," he added.

I sent a message to Matt telling him about our shortage of eighteen-gauge needles. I got a response the next day. A blood drive was to be held in Da Nang, and he and Joe were tapped to help out. He suggested Tom and I join them, since they needed help anyway, and we could pick up cartons of eighteen-gauge needles. Tom finagled permission for us to assist by promising this booty, plus the ship was heading to Da Nang at the same time as the blood drive.

A week later the *Repose* pulled into Da Nang Harbor, anchoring in the shadow of Monkey Mountain. We took a mike boat out to White Elephant Landing then caught a jeep to China Beach, an R&R spot set up to give guys a break without having to leave Vietnam. A white ribbon-shaped sign with "Welcome to China Beach" greeted us as we drove through the main gate and past a red and white-checkered water tank about three stories high.

Our driver dropped us at a square building with a red cross painted on its roof. It was a small aid station that took care of surfing injuries and minor maladies that struck the Marines at China Beach. Command had set up a couple of large tents around the building, which was where Tom and I found Matt and Joe and other corpsmen setting up blood-drawing tables. Soon, four hundred Marines descended on the area. I-Corps had provided a six-pack of free Pabst Blue Ribbon beer to those that donated blood, which was a good enough incentive for any GI. We stayed busy for two days, taking as much blood as the Marines could spare. Whole blood was always in short supply in a war zone.

The beer, it turned out, was not such a stellar idea. A Marine lacking a pint of blood and with a six-pack of beer makes for one helluva drunk GI. Fights broke out all over the place. Knocked out and passed out troops soon littered China Beach. In between blood drive duty, we also sutured cut-up Marines from the brawls and checked bodies for signs of life.

"Stupid isn't it," Tom said. "We come to China Beach to relax and yet knocking heads is all these dumb fucks can think of doing. I wonder if I can get a blowjob around here instead."

I guffawed and ran to Matt with an idea. The four of us, Matt, Joe, Tom and I, had spent the three nights together, eating and drinking and doing blood bank duty. We bunked in enlisted quarters, which comprised a row of metal-roofed buildings with eight bunks each.

On our second night we barbecued hamburgers under a stand of trees at the edge of the beach. Picnic tables with built-in benches were scattered about. Some tables were occupied, each containing small groups of men like ours.

"It's not all work, fellas," Matt said. "Let's hit the EM Club and make a night of it. Since this is our last day of blood drawing, I say we get us some beach time. I can fix it with the duty tech to get us off the roster for tomorrow."

The beach was wide with a constant supply of four-foot waves and a surfboard shop with cheap rentals. If surfing wasn't your thing, two guys could rent a small boat with a simple triangle sail and climb over the surf for a little quiet drifting offshore. Outboard motor boats were also available for rent. It was my definition of a sweet setup.

A short-lived television show portrayed a lot of white women working and living at China Beach, but I never saw any white women there. Local girls worked the PX, cafeteria, and bars. But the TV show was accurate in showing hundreds of men playing naked in the surf. We four members of The Group took in the sights.

Bobby joined us for our last afternoon and night. "I got the CO to give me an overnight chit off the ship. I ain't no green horn. I can work the system," he said when he arrived on the beach. Our last day, with no more Marines to bleed, we spent lolling on the shore's edge.

"Someday there'll be a big hotel right over there," Tom said, pointing to a nice spot down from us, "and over there will be a casino. You watch. We'll come back here on a gambling holiday and pine for the good times."

"Bullshit," Matt said. "This place will never be anything. Don't you get it, guys? These people are so backward they'll never buy into capitalism. This is a waste of lives what we're doing here. Hotels? Casinos? You gotta be fucking kidding me."

Matt did not believe in the war. The fact was, none of us believed in the mission. "Don't get me wrong, guys, I'm here because of them," Matt said, pointing to the men playing grab-ass in the surf. "It's for them that I haven't become an objector to this war. But you'll see. There will not and I repeat, not, be two separate Nams when we're done with this shit."

Joe agreed. "I don't ever want to come back. I've seen enough. This is not in my future, ever."

"What is in our future, you guys?" I said, trying to lighten the mood. "Look at all these beautiful men here." There were two to three hundred men cavorting on the beach. "Some of them have to be gay. We can't be the only ones."

Matt, always the smart one, spoke up with facts. "Kinsey's study says about thirty-five percent of men have been in bed with a man. According to him, about four to seven percent of all males on this planet are homos. I know what I want for my future."

I did some quick math in my head and determined at least eight other gay men must be on the beach. I scrutinized the surfers coming in on the waves, searching for them.

"I'm Catholic, so is Joe," Tom said. "I'm going to have to get married someday. That's the way the system is set up. 'Ozzie and Harriet' is the way it has to be if you don't want to be an outcast. I'll just have to have a secret life like we got here."

Joe looked at Tom. "Religion has shown me I'm not supposed to do anything with a guy, and I haven't, except for my sergeant because I don't want my life ruined. There won't be any future for us if we get caught. The Navy puts guys like us in jail, and it's on your record forever."

"I'm Catholic, too," Matt said. "I wish I was like David and never chose a religion."

"Our reality says none of us should be Runaround Sues," Tom joked.

The fear of discovery haunted all of us, and none of us talked about any exploits we may be having. The fear was too strong.

Bobby threw his hands in the air. "I don't know about you guys but my future is to find a husband, and I don't mean any of you bottom feeders. He'll be an officer, or my name isn't Kay-the-rich-bitch."

We laughed, defusing the tension. Truthfully, it never occurred to me to be on the prowl, and except for Matt, I wasn't going to bed anyone from The Group. We were sisters in the truest sense. The only time I would consider any sexual contact was on liberty. On ship or at the medical unit at Dong Ha was work, and I didn't play at work. That was the first time the thought of even the possibility of a husband, one person to settle down with, had come up in our talks.

Rather than admit that was what I wanted too, I said, "In your dreams, Kay. A husband? I can see you now in a bridal veil. Face it, we're outcasts, now and forever. I, for one, find comfort in that. Who wants to be milquetoast Ozzie anyway, or Harriet for that matter?"

"I wish for a future with a man," Matt said.

Later that night, we headed to the China Beach EM Club. It was an open-air affair. Matt and I sat at the bar, which had palm fronds that hung over our heads as we sipped drinks and talked. I assured Matt that nothing ever came from our getting caught kissing in Hong Kong. He laughed.

"That's what they call dodging a bullet," he said.

The others were talking to a bunch of Marines at a table next to the dance floor. "Those boys want to dance with them Marines in a bad way." He paused. "Changing the subject, I wanted to ask you something."

"Sure."

"Remember back in Dong Ha you said your dad beat you for being gay. How bad did it get?" Matt asked, sympathy evident in his eyes.

"He tried to kill me with a pipe wrench up the side of my head," I said. Matt's eyes widened. "That's when my mom finally kicked him out of the house. When he moved out, his last words to me were that he hated me and never loved me. I didn't care really. He was a colossal ass so whether he loved me or not didn't matter to me." My eyes shifted away from Matt's. I was trying not to show that my pain was the fact that I never really had a father, and maybe I wanted one.

"Sorry. I wish I could take away your sadness."

"My life wasn't all doom and gloom growing up," I continued. "My favorite uncles, my mother's brothers, Bobby and Rudy, and the husband of one of my aunts, Martin, are great guys. They love me a lot. Once they took me to Jerry's Place. It's a bar, what Mexicans call a cantina. There are eight women on that side of the family, and they needed a drink to get away from the sisters. I was five years old, but I remember Jerry's Place like it was yesterday."

"Where is it?" Matt asked.

"On the road between Salinas and Castroville, right in the middle of California. The Army boys from Fort Ord go there to have a swing with the whores."

"No bakla boys there, I bet," Matt said with a laugh.

"Hardly. But I remember Jerry's Place as being exciting. I love live music in small settings especially, I think, because of this one adventure in the cantina. The bar had a ranchero band that played polka-type music with a Mexican flair. I loved the energy and noise. The toot-toot-squeak-squeak from the brass instruments and the heavy-handed strumming of big stringed guitars, called *guitarones*, made a wonderful sound. *Braceros*, which means field workers, filled this place every night. They weren't allowed in other bars. Segregation between browns and whites is normal in my hometown. Prostitutes work the Army and Mexican guys every night. They make good money."

Matt giggled. "A healthy environment for a five-year-old."

I related the story of how one particularly bodacious prosty knelt down to look me in the eye and said "*m'ijo*, you are so cute." Then she asked my uncles, "May I take him?" They laughed and told her yes.

"She proceeded to carry me around the bar telling everyone I was her baby. I loved it. The attention was fun. Her tits were enormous and soft. I fit comfortably between them as she carried me around. I vividly remember she was wearing a white dress with a pattern of huge polka dots of different colors. The hem of the dress was scalloped. To me it was the most beautiful evening gown I'd seen."

"What happened? Something must have happened for you to remember all those details," Matt said. He was so interested in my story that my heart ached for him to love me.

"All of a sudden, a guy ran in and yelled, "*Cuidado, el jefe!*" Spanish for 'watch it, the boss.' Everyone in the bar turned and looked at Bodacious and me. She runs to my uncle's table and put me under it. Then she called over a couple of other prosties. They grabbed chairs and crowded around the table as if talking to my handsome uncles. Two jack-booted marshals, handsome, beautiful, masculine men in uniform, walked in. I was in awe as I peeked out from under the table. I only caught glimpses of their faces. I didn't know why I was hiding, but I knew better than to say anything or move. They walked around all cop-like and as they got near our little table, the girls all spread their legs to hide the underside of the table. Guess what? None of them wore underwear. I swear to god, they looked like they had big black spiders pasted between their legs."

Matt laughed so hard that I wrapped my arm around him to keep him from falling off the bar stool. "What the fuck happened?" he wailed.

"I started to giggle, then one of my uncles kicked me. I shut up until the marshals finally left. My uncles immediately began to argue. 'You stupid, why did we bring the kid?' 'What do you mean?' Rudy said, 'you brought him. Rachael could lose the baby because of your stupid idea.'"

Matt really was enjoying my story and leaned his head on my shoulder still laughing his ass off. "How many times did you go to Jerry's Place?" he asked.

"I never went back," I answered.

The rest of The Group walked in.

"What are you guys laughing so hard about?" Bobby said.

I said something about it being a long story as we left to sleep off the night's drinking.

Bobby, Tom, and I caught a chopper back to the ship that morning, and we carried several large boxes of 18-gauge needles.

Matt and Joe hitched a ride on a C-46 Commando, a small aircraft used for in-country travel, for their trip back to Dong Ha.

CHAPTER TEN

The War of 1967

Nine more months duty on the *Repose* could never be described as bad; my stint on the beach was more difficult. But those months stretched across a time warp that felt like two years. After Hong Kong, the ship stayed on station for a month, and then returned to Subic Bay in February 1967 for a week of R&R and resupply.

An election for the mayor of Olongapo City was going on during that time, and we learned a lot about the Filipino democratic process.

Olongapo was in a strange situation. The rest of the Philippines had been granted independence from the United States on July 4, 1946. Olongapo, however, remained under U.S. government jurisdiction. It had been declared a U.S. Naval Reservation soon after the United States and Spain signed the Treaty of Paris. This jurisdiction status was the last piece of the Spanish-American War agreement to fall into place. It stipulated that a U.S. Navy officer was in charge, which effectively made him the leader of Olongapo's government. The Filipinos still held political campaigns and elections, but the reality was the military assigned the position no matter the outcome of the vote.

Residents of the base had to follow strict rules—carrying an ID card issued by the Reservation office; homes could not be owned and could be taken back at any time by the Navy; out-of-town relatives could only stay for a few days and had to renew their passes if extending their stay; only families with members working for the Navy could reside in the Reservation.

The Filipinos long resented the regulations, but they grew angry when more rules were implemented. To get on and off the base, Filipinos used a Navy bus service. Now their belongings were going to undergo a complete search. On February 20, 1967, Nonito Alincastre, a fugitive escapee from the national penitentiary, gunned down the military's handpicked candidate for mayor, James Leonard Tagle Gordon. His father was American but he himself was a citizen of the Philippines. The local political structure felt Gordon was too closely tied to the Americans. To me, Alincastre was being set up as the fall guy for an ulterior plan to push the Americans out.

The *Repose* was moored along the shore. I watched the wounded Gordon brought aboard from the deck rail outside my ward. I knew a dead man when I saw one. He succumbed to his wounds immediately after his arrival. Such was life in port aboard the Angel of the Orient.

————— ◆ —————

The Group gathered every night at Club Oro and hung out with our girlfriends, the lady boys. Because they were so beautiful, none of the surrounding servicemen in the bar suspected a thing.

"How you doing, Vangie? Making good money?" I asked my girlfriend one night as we settled at the table with our drinks.

"I have a daddy who pays for my own apartment. It's nice and he likes me the way I am."

I was happy she had someone taking care of her. "Good. I know it can be dangerous for you. I worry about you."

She then gave me a Christmas present that she'd been waiting for me to get into port to give to me. It was a forty-five record of "Born Free."

"'Born Free' is now my favorite record. Sorry, I don't have anything for you."

"That's okay. You're nice. I like that you don't push me for good time."

The next day, the ship prepared to get underway. The call went out for all hands below E-5 to get stores aboard. It was hard physical work, especially in the oppressive humidity. Some of the corpsmen would ditch out of this, but I liked to help bring the food onto the ship. A hundred men lined the decks and down the ladders all the way to the hold area, six decks below, to create a human chain of passing goods. The humidity made me hate every second of the work and I wished I had ditched, but it had to be done.

At one point, a five-foot-long roll of cured ground meat in a casing was handed to me. I realized where the term "horse-cock" came from, and why the cook used that word to describe bologna sandwiches.

The month of March and ten days of April saw the ship on duty, about six weeks at sea. We never knew our schedule. The battles in the field dictated how long we stayed off the coast taking wounded. It was a frenzied couple of months, both on the ship and ashore.

———— ◆ ————

"Flight quarters, flight quarters," whispered the speakers of the 1MC, the ship's intercom system, in the usual nighttime voice used to wake up the corpsmen. I checked the time. It was 0210. "Prepare for thirty ambulatory and forty litter patients."

Fifteen corpsmen on the duty roster were normally assigned to flight quarters, but usually only a dozen showed up. Some were busy with something else. This time, though, I made out in the darkness of our sleeping area many corpsmen rising in their racks, like vampires lifting themselves for their ghoulish prowling.

"What did it just say?" whispered Bobby from his bunk across from me.

"Forty litter patients," I whispered back.

I got up and joined Bobby and about twenty-five other corpsmen making our way topside. We all knew it was going to take more than the duty crew to handle the wounded tonight.

It was windy, and that made landing by the choppers tricky. Imagine a windmill on a farm coming off in a tornado and heading your way. That's what it felt like when the copters landed on deck.

Two bright lights of the landing aircraft broke through the darkness. At that instant, it seemed as if the moon were dropping on top of us. A vivid tingling of fear ran through my body. It was dangerous on deck when flights came in. A million things could go wrong with helicopters landing on what could only be described as a makeshift-landing pad on the ship's stern. A whoop whoop whoop sound from the chopper rotors added to equipment rattle, making it impossible to hear.

Two ramps led to the pad from both sides of the ship. On the starboard side, we corpsmen stood waiting for the flight officer to signal us to evac patients from the Hueys or Chinooks. If the officer held his fingers up, the patients were ambulatory and required one corpsman each to take to triage. If he pointed his fingers down, they were stretchers, which required two men to carry. If two litters were on board the helo, he pointed four fingers down to indicate the number of men needed. The noise of the blades was loud and constant.

The Chinooks usually held no more than five to six walking wounded, and at most four litter patients. But that night the first Chinook that landed held eight stretchers and a bunch of walking wounded. I didn't know how they fitted them in.

With the ramps narrow, it would be impossible for so many men to make their way down them. Flight crew and ship crew pulled the stretchers out and positioned them for us corpsmen to carry.

The windmill of the blades was wheeling above us at a crazy speed. The choppers stayed revved full-on in case an emergency lift-off was necessary. We approached the insane flywheel, the blades spinning above, bent at the hip. Our heads weren't tall enough to touch the moving blades; it was one of those things we did by instinct.

I was at the front. The officer in charge ran to me.

"Corpsman!" the flight officer shouted in my ear. "There are six stretcher cases on this one and seven walking! We'll do the stretchers first!"

That was the first time the officer on the landing pad had ever addressed me. The number of casualties was unprecedented for the Chinook that had just landed. It had obviously been a battle that had gone badly.

I could not indicate with two hands that twelve men were needed to the men behind me. Instead, I grabbed Bobby who had gone up with me and was standing behind me, and pulled him past myself and pushed him toward the chopper. Then I indicated with two hands that ten more men were needed. I followed them to the waiting copter.

The triage area held only nine stretchers. They would need to use the interior passageway outside the triage area for other incoming cases. I didn't have time to think about that; this first stretcher held a man who needed immediate help.

"Doctor, this guy is bad and more are coming in. What do we do?" I asked the surgeon who had triage responsibility.

We had no time to do the usual sorting protocol, just too many damned wounded.

The doctor took one glance at the man. The entire left side of his face was blown off; his left arm and leg were missing. Part of his skull was ripped open. "Good god. Take him down to pre-op. They'll have to decide. Alert them that I'll need to send others, too," the surgeon said.

Normally a patient with such severe injuries would have been triaged out for not having much of a chance of living. But there was no time to make that determination. Bobby and I took him down to the elevator that went six decks below to the surgery suites and Tom's area in pre-op.

This below-ship area, the bottom really, was the steadiest part of the *Repose*. In rolling seas, no doctor wanted to attempt delicate scalpel cuts on an operating table located on any of the upper decks.

"These guys must be coming directly from a dust-off. They've only had a minimum of work done," I said between grunts as Bobby and I carried the man.

Bobby looked down at the tag the field corpsman had attached. "He's been given morphine, and he's got just compression bandages on his open stumps. The shit must have hit the fan if the guys at Dong Ha weren't able to do more."

You could OD a patient on morphine if those tags weren't in place, I thought.

We got the man onto a gurney in post-op. Bobby moved off to help one of the surgeons work on a guy set for his operation. I was left alone with the double amputee.

Tom gave me instructions until the doctor arrived. The guy had multiple packing wraps around the stumps of his arm and leg. They were soaked with blood but couldn't be changed.

"Leave the packing in place or he'll bleed out," Tom spoke in a rush of words but confidently. He knew his shit, and I needed him right now.

"He has an IV of plasma already going. Should I switch out for whole blood?" I asked him.

"No, leave it. He's got to get more fluids in him if he's going to have a chance."

The man still had portions of his uniform on. I got to work cutting off the remaining parts of his greens. Tom went and grabbed some O Pos blood. There was no time for a cross match.

"David, get to work on a cutdown on the femoral artery in the groin area of the good leg and pump this blood into him as soon as you get the IV tube set," Tom said.

Using one of the new 18-gauge needles we'd procured, I performed the procedure quickly.

Tom pulled off the shreds of the Marine's trousers. His testicles and penis had been blown away, too.

"How is this guy still alive?" I said as the shakes took hold of me.

The plasma ran out. Tom put in dextrose and saline in the IV instead.

"Man, we need to get blood into this guy," Tom said. His jaw was clenched. The cover of the IV bottle was in his mouth as he had pulled it out with his teeth to be able to connect it quickly with both hands to the IV tube.

A doctor rushed over. "This man is in tachycardia with possible cardiac arrest coming on, Corpsman," he told me. "Administer two mg of epinephrine and two cc of lidocaine, stat." He rushed to a new patient being brought in.

Tom quickly set up a syringe with the drugs and handed it to me. "Does this guy even want to live?" he asked as he hurried to another side of the room.

I remembered thinking the same thing when I watched the training films of multiple amputees from the Korean War.

The doctor returned. "Remove the bandages from his stump and clamp off the bleeders. Be quick or he'll die in seconds," he directed.

I removed the compress bandages covering his stump; he was missing his leg to three inches above the knee. He had a tourniquet, but that wasn't sufficient to stop the blood from squirting out of the femoral artery. An instrument tray appeared. Bobby had known what would be necessary before I could say it, and Tom came to help.

Using the first clamp I found in the tray, I pinched off the largest artery. Next, Tom used hemostats on other bleeding vessels. Another bottle of blood and another plasma bag were handed to me.

"Doctor Stern!" Tom called out. "I think we need to stop here."

The ordering doctor came over, did a pulse check and stethoscope sounding. He looked up at me and nodded.

The man had died in my hands. I immediately squirreled that into the little Pandora's box in my brain.

Because a corpsman's job also required ID checking, a tooth-plotting chart needed to be done on the deceased, as well as cleaning and whip-stitching any wounds or organ cavity openings. Bobby and I spent the next fifteen minutes readying him for tagging and bagging. We did this at lighting speed; the wounded were still flowing in.

———— • ————

Bobby and I took a shower at around 0730 in the night-quarters area, the hold part of the ship where Tom lived. Blood mixed with dirt covered our arms and clothes. It wasn't just mud. A chemical smell saturated the uniforms we stripped off the wounded. It was a defoliant the chemical company Monsanto had sold to the military to clear vegetation off mountaintops. It was sticky and stunk. We inhaled it every time men were brought direct from the field. It always left me with a heavy chest for a couple days. It was called Agent Orange.

After showering, I reported to the nurse on my ward for my 0800 shift.

"Lara, you don't look so good. I know what's gone down. You take off for the day. Get some shuteye. We have it covered here," she said.

The nurses were generally hard-assed toward us, but her eyes held only sympathy this time. I hit the rack. I didn't have a thought in my head, but I went to sleep with the moans, screams, yells and sobs of injured men echoing in my head. There was no way to shut that off. Thoughts, I could turn off, but sounds, I couldn't control.

———— • ————

On April 2, 1967, the USS *Sanctuary* (AH-17) joined the 7th Fleet at Subic Bay. Eight days later, she arrived at Da Nang and that afternoon took her first casualties. She was a floating hospital just like ours. When we looked at her, it was like looking in a mirror. The *Sanctuary* was an exact replica of our white-painted ship with red crosses on its sides.

The *Sanctuary's* arrival allowed the *Repose* to head into dock to get a needed overhaul. On April 11, we set out to the Philippines and were to remain there until April 26 while we were outfitted with new water evaporators and equipment was repaired.

Don and KC had remained my friends despite their realization that I was gay. No one was fooled by the pretense that gays didn't exist in the Navy. Living in such close quarters, shipmates figured it out but no one cared. Do your job, don't fuck around (figuratively and literally) and no one gave a shit. Still, that didn't mean you were safe. Piss someone off and they had the sword that allowed them to end your career in the military. The threat of prison and a dishonorable discharge never changed. Keeping our heads down and doing a better job than other corpsmen were the only things that assured us some safety.

KC came over to my bunk one day while we were in port. "Hey, Lara. Don, Voss, Garcia, and a couple of the other guys from Corps School are going over to Grande Island. There's a hotel that charges just a couple of dimes a night. We're planning on staying two nights. Plus the EM club has a great floorshow. Want to join us for a class reunion?"

"Hell yeah," I said. "I want to check out the Jap gun emplacements I heard some swabbies from the *Okinawa* talk about. They're bigger than Howitzers. There's even an observation tower that gives a bitchin' view of Subic Bay."

The USS *Okinawa* was an amphibious assault ship, and I had seen it in port on our last time at Subic. I remembered that Scott, my sailor trick I had when I was sixteen, had told me he was stationed aboard her. A few nights ago, I had found guys from her at the Club Oro and spent a night of drinking and bullshitting, but I had little hope of finding my sailor. I wanted to be close to his shipmates anyway so I struck up a conversation with the sailors when I heard they were from the *Okinawa*.

"You guys know anyone aboard named Scott?" I asked.

"Not really," replied the corpsman assigned to the *Okinawa* that I was drinking with. "We're almost a carrier so there's a shitload of men aboard. Plus, who in the Navy calls each other by their first name?"

I laughed at the obvious truth of his statement. I did not have Scott's last name so I gave up my search.

The next day my Corps School group and I hopped a mike boat and headed out into Subic Bay and to Grande Island at the mouth of the harbor for two nights of baseball, sky larking, World War II history studies, drinking, and sunbathing on the tiny beaches of this fortress island.

At the time, the Navy offered history lessons on various World War II battles or operation areas that sailors could complete for promotion credit. Fort Wint was an old base on the island. Since it was mentioned in a lesson, I took the tour.

The fort had been armed with fourteen Taft-Endicott period coastal artillery pieces mounted in five batteries. Battery Warwick contained the fort's most powerful weaponry, two 12-inch M1895MI disappearing guns mounted on Buffington Crozier carriages. Batteries Hall and Woodruff each mounted two 6-inch M1905 guns, also on disappearing carriages. Batteries Flake and Jewell were armed with 3-inch M1903 guns on pedestal mounts. As with other forts of the same period, Fort Wint's weaponry was obsolete by the outbreak of hostilities with Japan in 1941. This lesson explained away the notion that the Japanese used them during World War II. It was fun stuff to learn, and if it helped me to advance, I was willing to do the extra work.

That afternoon our gang went swimming on one of the tiny beaches. I needed a little alone time and walked by myself around the shore of the small island. I spotted a group of sailors swimming nude around the bend from where my classmates were.

Nude bathing was not considered provocative. Sailors saw each other naked all the time, so it was no big whoop for a bunch of guys doffing their clothes for a bit of skinny dipping.

As I approached them, I realized I had found Scott, my sailor from San Diego. He stood in the water watching his friends swim and turned as I got near. His eyes squinted and his smile widened when he realized it was me. The feeling of a pleasant surprise was a moment of happiness that I'd not felt in a long time. Scott was as handsome as I remembered. I strode up to him as a sailor and an equal.

"Fancy seeing you here. You joined the Navy," he said. It was as if it was the most natural thing to have encountered each other. We sat down laughing a bit about the coincidence.

"Let me get this straight. You joined up at seventeen, like me?" he asked.

I explained about my mom's death and how a court order made me an adult. I didn't know it but his situation was pretty much the same. His naked buddies, three other sailors, were his "Group" that he formed on the *Okinawa*. He was stationed on her from the time we met and had re-upped on the ship. So this encounter, while improbable in the grand scheme of things, was not impossible.

"It was less than a year after you and I had that great night together in San Diego that I joined up," I said. "I've seen the *Okinawa* in Da Nang harbor and sailing near us a few times since I've been aboard the *Repose*. I've thought of you each time. How's duty on her?"

"We operate off the coast in the same area you guys do. You can't miss the *Repose*. I've spotted your ship often. The *Okinawa* acts as a mobile base with Marines that are better equipped than the troops on patrol in-country. It's the high-powered equipment that the ground troops are missing so our Marines have that equipment and can strike via helicopters in support of ground forces. We cover the same Phu Bai, Chu Lai and Dong Ha areas of operation that the *Repose* works."

I didn't introduce his group to my gang, since mine was not gay and his was. That would have put a damper on his group's time away from the straight world.

"Why don't you meet me at Landing Cover by Cubi Point next Sunday at 1500, and I'll take you on a tour of the *Okinawa*," Scott suggested. "See if you can get the night off. The Navy Airbase at Cubi has a nice hotel with private rooms. We can spend the night together." He winked, and I nodded.

I met Scott as arranged. We had our secret date, with him showing me where he worked and lived. Afterward, he changed into his dress whites to match mine. I wanted to look good for him. We left for dinner; he'd made reservations at the Cubi Point Airbase Officers' Club.

"All of us on-board the *Okinawa* have access to the officers' club because of our aircraft capability. It's a courtesy the flying officers' organization gives enlisted that serve on aircraft carriers," Scott said.

The club was located on a high bluff overlooking the Cubi Point airstrip, which sat on the edge of the opening to Subic Bay.

"It's beautiful here, thanks for working this for us," I said after we ordered drinks and dinner. "I really liked meeting your friends today. I've formed my own group of gays. We jokingly call ourselves The Group, named for a movie we've all have seen."

"Not familiar with it. I'll have to catch it someday." Scott smiled and touched my knee under the table.

"Two guys from my ship and two corpsmen stationed at the aid station at Dong Ha are part of my group. I work there sometimes when the Navy deems it necessary to assign me on shore."

"You've seen combat then?" Scott asked.

"Not actual humping in the jungle, but I've been at Dong Ha when the rockets fly in. The ship gets men directly from the field. Sometimes I think it's worse being on the ship. I see a lot of wounded and dying. But I wouldn't be anywhere else." I decided not to continue that line of conversation. "Besides I have my group and that makes it easier."

"At first I was afraid of making homo friends even though I could spot the guys aboard my ship easy enough," Scott said. "But I figure, what the fuck? I need guys I can talk to about real stuff and not be a big phony all the time." He seemed sad.

"Why are you down?" I asked.

Scott gave a melancholy smile. "I broke a rule I made for myself and fell in love with a shipmate."

"Not a good idea. I make sure to turn off that part of me that wants a man while onboard or at the base. I literally look at a man I am attracted to and shut down any idea of sex or relationship. It's difficult, but I can see how someone like you and me could slip up. But why the sad mouth?"

Scott seemed as if he was going to cry. "He was turned in by someone. There wasn't any real evidence. The Navy decided in its mind that smoke meant fire. They chucked him out with a dishonorable discharge."

"That's tough."

"The real tough thing is they had no evidence. It was just an accusation. They offered him a way out if he would name any homosexuals aboard the ship that he might know." Scott's eyes welled with tears. "He wouldn't do it. Not to me, and not to any of the guys you met yesterday either. I loved him."

"Do you write to him?" I asked looking at him with all the sympathy I could share.

"I lost track of him. I know he ended up at Treasure Island in San Francisco for processing. But I've never gotten a letter or address. I heard his family told him to never come home. I have no way of finding him."

There was no sense in kidding ourselves about having a relationship. How can two people in the Navy, gay or not, have an ongoing commitment when their ships will eventually head in different directions? But a night together at the Cubi Point Hotel was doable. Scott and I spent the night and morning making love with no commitments. We didn't even exchange addresses after saying goodbye the next morning. There was no point. My ship was due out in two days, and the USS *Okinawa* was soon to head back to her homeport of San Diego. That was our reality and we were fine with it. I did ask him his last name this time just in case I bumped into anyone from the *Okinawa* again. But I never saw the ship or Scott again.

———◆———

At the end of April 1967, the *Repose* departed for another long stretch on station off the coast of Vietnam. As we made our way back to war, I turned nineteen at sea. I was a man in every way possible. The night with Scott proved that, if nothing else. My biological age meant nothing.

CHAPTER ELEVEN

A Sinking

We weren't always taking on battlefield casualties. A few times we had quiet moments while anchored in Da Nang Harbor. The sick still came aboard, but they were general medical patients, those usually destined for my ward on A-deck. They had fevers and ailments that came from the crazy variety of pathogens that a steamy wet jungle had to offer.

The wounded had already undergone preliminary treatment at one of the military med stations in Da Nang so they came aboard without the frantic activity of flight quarters and triage.

We only docked at the deep-water pier once while in Da Nang. Normally, we stayed anchored in the bay, not far from Monkey Mountain. When we were on station off Dong Ha, on the other hand, the ship sailed around in circles because the waters were too deep for anchoring. But in the harbor, we dropped anchor and the *Repose* would lazily drift around in circles depending on the tide and winds.

During the day, when crew and corpsmen were off duty, we hung out on the uppermost deck of the ship, the O2 level. Patients used this deck, too. It had a shuffleboard feel as one might find on a cruise ship. On the *Repose*, we used it for movies at night and for general lolling about on hot, humid days. Card playing was the normal pastime.

I had purchased a small Third Man Crosley record player in Subic. It measured about four by seven by twelve inches. It looked like a shoebox and had a yellowish Bakelite body with built-in speakers in the bottom half, as well as battery chambers. The top had the pulley system that drove the record around for playing. A thin swing arm stylus completed the system, which could play 45s and 33 LP records. It had a remarkably good sound, or maybe I only thought so since I couldn't remember any other record players on the ship. I started a small collection of 45s and even a few 33s, one being the soundtrack from "The Sound of Music." My favorite 45 was "Born Free," the one given to me by Vangie, my ersatz girlfriend in Olongapo.

The day was hot and still and the water glass smooth as the ship lay anchored in Da Nang Bay. I was playing records and looking over the rail, watching sea snakes play around the edge of our ship. They were ugly, five-foot-long, white serpents that evolved from some land-bound ancestor millions of years ago. Over the millennia, they had adapted to aquatic life and were unable to move on land. They were also venomous, but generally didn't bite humans unless harassed. They had a paddle-like tail with the body laterally compressed down their sides, which gave them an eel-like appearance. This evolutionary adaptation allowed for locomotion in the water. It was creepy to watch them swim. Unlike eels, they did not have gills and had to surface regularly to breathe.

Patients and some crew congregated around my record player for a few tunes. The ambulatory patients generally wore their green utility pants and a blue hospital top when they moved around the ship. They didn't wear hospital gowns as in stateside hospitals. Instead, we provided them with pajama-type outfits made of medium blue cotton with drawstring bottoms. The strings didn't hold up shit so the guys who were truly ambulatory wore their green utility trousers.

Suddenly, I saw that configuration of clothing topple over the rail and into the water. One of my patients had just jumped overboard. Training took over. "Man overboard! Man overboard!" I screamed.

I kept up the call while grabbing a life ring hanging on a bulkhead next to me. I threw it towards the guy, and the klaxon signaling man overboard blared throughout the ship. A lifeboat crew unhitched a boat hanging next to me. It and crew went over the rail and made for the guy, who was treading water below us using the ring I had thrown. Once I saw they had him, I went to my ward. I had recognized him.

"Dr. Dubois, one of your patients just went over the side. I know the guy, Jenkins. Jerome is his first name. I think we need to get the psych doctor."

"I'll call down and get one up here. Do you know what might be up?"

"He may be shell-shocked. I've had night duty, and he has nightmares where he yells out."

Dr. Dubois trusted my judgment and didn't ask for details. He grabbed the ship's phone as I left the office.

As Jenkins was brought into A-deck ward, I got one of the private-patient rooms in the officer's ward ready along with Nurse Hildebrand. She'd made the call to put Jenkins in a room by himself. I sat the Marine on the bed to remove his wet clothing.

"I can't go back. I can't go back in the shit," he mumbled. He was scheduled to return to duty soon.

Dubois stood at the open door. As he turned to leave he said, "Stay with him, Lara."

I stayed and talked to him quietly. "You don't want to go back into combat?"

He said he couldn't take it anymore.

"Why did you jump overboard?" I asked.

"I got to get back to my unit," he said in a deadpan voice.

He didn't know what he was saying. He'd snapped. It was a one-way ticket home. His confusion was due to his duty he felt to his brothers in the field but his mind was unable to fight anymore. Every day I grew more skeptical of our reason to be in this conflict. Things like this only enforced my growing antiwar sentiment.

I sat murmuring soothing words and wishing there was good psychiatric help available, but I was dubious. I expected things wouldn't work out well for him. I hated to be the voice of doom, but I felt that this war would not sit well with any of us mentally. Nobody would escape totally sane. The only question for each of us was, how deeply damaged would we be? Only time would answer that question.

It was the middle of May, and we soon left Da Nang Harbor to start another month of operation off the coast. The battlefield called and we answered. The routine of midnight flight quarters with the never-ending rotary thunder of dark windy nights topside returned.

I didn't feel numb to what I was seeing and doing, but I had to control my empathy and emotions or I would be the one jumping overboard. Burned and bleeding, screaming in pain or unconscious near-death, men came every other night, it seemed. Not large numbers but constant. Ten here, five there, walking or stretcher. It didn't stop, and I didn't stop to think about it.

Our duty, and that included all aboard the USS *Repose*, was clear. We did it without thinking. Get the job done. Do it and do it now! No hesitation. Keep going because a new round was coming. That dedication to duty stayed with us every moment while on station. The routine consisted of treating the men, easing their suffering, and putting them to bed in clean sheets with the hope of quieting their fears. Sometimes that routine was broken in peculiar and almost entertaining ways.

"Underway replenishment or UNREP," said my deck ape friend Bubbles, as if lecturing a new recruit, "is an at-sea method of transferring fuel, munitions, and stores from one ship to another while underway."

Bubbles was doing paint duty next to me while I stood watching the roaring deep blue sea that churned between our ship and one running next to us at high speed. He had smears of white paint on his wrist and nose because he was applying the chalky paint that made up the color of our Albino Bitch. He had a squint to his eyes from the reflection of sun off the bright white paint. I had asked him a question on how the operation we were undertaking was going to go down.

Bubbles pointed to the other ship and continued a lecture he had obviously received from some boatswain's mate in the past. "The alongside connected replenishment or CONREP, is the equipment we use for transferring liquids such as fuel and fresh water from a supply ship."

We stood at the rail on the O2 level watching as the supply ship pulled alongside us. "The supply ship holds a steady course and speed, generally between twelve and sixteen knots. Moving at this speed lessens relative motion from wave action and allows better control of the ship's heading. As the receiving ship, we are coming alongside now. We keep a distance of about forty yards."

Not quite a half a football field's length, I thought.

Then I heard loud pop. A gun-line, or pneumatic line thrower, went off from the supply ship as they fired cables to our ship's forecastle where *Repose* deck hands waited. It was obviously a pull line of some sort.

"You see that?" Bubbles pointed. "That coming over now is a phone line for voice communication and the transfer rig lines."

I learned that as the command ship of the replenishment operation, they provided all lines and equipment needed for the transfer of our fuel and water. On occasion, packaged supplies were also moved between ships, and even people, in a chair-like carrier, could ride over.

It was June 15, and suddenly everything went awry. The USS *Misspillion* (AO-105), a fleet auxiliary tanker, was transferring fuel when our aft steering pin snapped. All the angles began to change. I saw masts where they should not have been, and our bow was moving in the wrong direction. As Bubbles and I stood topside, the akimbo shifting of familiar ship parts scared the shit out of us.

In slow motion, we turned into the midsection of the tanker with our bow. I was knocked to the deck from the force of the impact. Bubbles had hold of the rail and remained standing, and then he ran to the ladder near us and descended, heading in the direction of the bow.

"General quarters," called over our PA systems. We were taking on water. Abandoning ship became a real possibility.

I jumped up and hurried in the direction my buddy had just gone because I could hear yelling. As I looked down at the forecastle, crewmen were lying all over the deck. The tanker was still right in front of us, but I didn't register the danger of that juxtaposition. I slid down the ladder and checked the injured.

The tanker then backed up to get away from us, and all hell broke loose. The capstan that held the ropes and transfer rigging, which were basically big rubber-hoses, broke and fell on us. Everyone scrambled for cover.

Someone yelled, "Clear the forecastle!"

The capstan was a huge metal mast and had all kinds of heavy rigging attached. Bubbles and I grabbed one of the injured guys and ran. But the way was blocked by others fleeing and we couldn't get away in time. A large piece of the rigging fell on the three of us. Luckily, I only sustained a sprained ankle. Bubbles wasn't injured and the hurt guy didn't suffer any additional wounds. Others weren't as lucky. One man died when the capstan broke in half and toppled onto him, crushing his head.

After things quieted I couldn't help but think that we would probably head for Japan for repairs, which I wouldn't mind at all. Sailors are a cynical lot. Men were injured and I was thinking "oh goody, Yokosuka here we come." Unfortunately, that didn't happen.

"KC, have you heard? We're TDY'd to White Elephant Landing in Da Nang while the *Repose* goes to Subic Bay for repairs."

I was packing my sea bag when he entered our bunk area. I was the first to give him the bad news. "It'll take about three and a half weeks."

"Motherfucker," he muttered in his southern drawl.

Our orders stipulated that we would get temporary duty, or TDY'd, onto the beach. This wasn't a real surprise to us. That was our job; KC, Don and myself knew this would happen. But boy, was it a disappointment. We'd miss out on almost a month in Subic.

Later, KC turned to me as we hopped a chopper to the beach. "I guess that's the perks we get for being dual-service trained. To the beach, Lara, to the beach we go."

———— ◆ ————

At the end of June, I got to do my first "county fair" while I hung out in Da Nang while the ship enjoyed dry dock in Subic. I love the term "county fair." It was a combination of military, civic, and psychological warfare action designed to reestablish the Vietnamese government's control over a given area, or, so the SOPs said.

"Mr. Lara," said a Marine officer, "this is an activity designed to flush the Viet Cong from a community in which they have become a parasite on the populace. It's designed to ensure that the populace is not alienated against the war effort or the South Vietnamese duly elected government." He delivered this with a stoic, John Wayne face. "You'll help us implement this military action in your capacity as a medical person as we attempt to convince the population that the government is interested in the welfare of the people and that the government's victory over the Viet Cong is inevitable."

"Yeah, right," I muttered to his retreating back after he informed me that I was to join the 9th Marines' "bullshit" operation, as I called it.

A Marine combat unit cordoned off the target area, a village or hamlet, in order to isolate it for the duration of the county fair, and then the corpsmen provided limited medical treatment to the people. The Marines also had their duties, such as speaking to the village elders or entertaining the children with gum and candy.

The area was in the middle of some rice paddies south of Da Nang near a cluster of large hills literally made of marble. We knew Charlie hid in them. But it was a fucking waste to try and blow them out of there. These mountains, really just hills, were near the American Marble Mountain Air Facility. I had been here before because I'd landed at the airfield a few times already and gone to China Beach, which bordered the airfield. I had no idea which side of Marble Mountain this village was on. In fact, most of my time in-country I didn't know where I was on a map. I just knew it was dangerous.

We traveled by road on M-561 Gamma Goat Trucks, six-wheeled semi-amphibious vehicles that could pass through wet areas easily. To enter the village, we had to hump in. The team and I walked along half-foot-high bunds that separated the square, shallow-watered rice fields. The village was literally a high and dry island in the middle of rice paddies. They had graded the tiny mound so that rain drained into the paddies. It was dusty as we marched in, passing the ubiquitous grass-thatch roofed huts the locals lived in. To keep the interiors dry, the huts sat on stilts, two feet off the ground. I'd already seen some huts near Dong Ha that were quite high, maybe five feet off the ground, but those were in areas that became flooded any time a hard rain came, which was often in the "suck."

Walking in, I passed water buffalo used to till the fields. They looked big and unpleasant. I especially disliked their black, mucus-smeared noses. The beasts had the annoying habit of sticking out an ugly purple tongue to lick their unlovely noses. I passed a wrinkled old woman holding a baby that was maybe a year old. I looked down into a basket beside her and halted. It contained black-horned beetles. They were three inches long, arranged in a row, and twice the width of a quarter. She laughed at my curious study with a wide mouth, and her jaw shifted slightly left, making it look like an old coin purse with loose teeth in it.

The old woman took out a beetle, putting it to her teeth like a pirate testing a doubloon to see if it were real gold. "Chop chop baby san number one," she said in a crackling voice, indicating that they fed the innards of these monsters to babies. These people were going to need lots of medical attention just for the parasites they were ingesting.

My "propaganda medicine" mission included inoculations for measles and smallpox, removal of splinters, and cleaning of debris from wounds the rural villagers always had. Wounds became infected easily in the humidity. I did some simple suturing of deep cuts, too.

I worked on a fourteen-year-old kid who had inflamed insect bites on his legs. A couple of South Vietnamese soldiers who'd accompanied us were our interpreters.

"Tell the kid to put this ointment on his legs after washing them at night for three days," I told the interpreter. The cortisone ointment was specially made to work in the tropics with a base of heavy petroleum jelly. The head corpsman told me the natives responded well to our treatments, such as antibiotics, because their bodies were naive to this stuff. "Give them only short duration treatment instructions," he said. "Hell, usually they stop before finishing the medication and sell the rest anyway, but they will heal even with incomplete treatment."

The kid looked at me as I wrapped up. "You go now?" he asked, as our crew packed up. We were done here.

"Yeah, Charlie-san, we di-di now," I said, using slang and the native word for leaving or going.

"You number one, Bac Si Joe," said the kid.

I looked at my interpreter with a questioning eye. "He says you're the best doctor."

I smiled and patted him on the head. "You number one too, Charlie-san."

I kept a picture that a Marine took with the kid and me. I always wondered if the boy was on our side or the VC's. I would never know.

The smells were foul in these villages. They used the water buffalo dung as fertilizer, which made sense. But they had the habit of mixing it with a little fermented human excrement, known as night soil.

Hence, unpleasant odors emanated from the area where night soil was composted. Hiking back to our pickup area, we passed a pit of this warm shit. Ooof!

———◆———

I flew up to Dong Ha to work a couple of nights before the *Repose* returned from dry dock. I got to hang out with the combat part of The Group.

"Hey Matt, Joe, how ya doin', boys?"

"Yo, look what the rat dragged in," Matt said.

That really wasn't a joke because there were some humongous rats running around that actually could have dragged me in. One night one ran across my chest. It was a heavy bitch that knocked the wind out of me.

Matt and Joe hugged and slapped me affectionately. I sat them down with some exciting news.

"I got word that the *Repose* is going to Singapore for a few R&R days. So work your magic, Matt, tell them that you heroes deserve a flight and a few days in Singapore. I really want to get The Group together for one last time before we go back to the world. We're expected to dock at the British Naval Base HMS Terror on August 7."

Matt agreed. "I forget that all five of The Group are now short-timers."

"Just get you and Ski there somehow." I put my arm around Matt while patting the top of his head and kissing his sweet mouth. "I'm only getting one night with you boys. The *Repose* comes back on station tomorrow. It was patched up good, according to Tom. He's anxious to see you."

Then it was back to work. I hopped aboard a Chinook full of wounded from a fire fight that happened the day before at the Razorback area near Khe Sahn. Jungle warfare was a filthy hell. The bandages were filled with the red mud of the foxholes these men were dragged out of, a red different from the color of blood. I was becoming tired of looking at these. I wanted to go home, even if I had no home to go back to.

By now, I thought I was used to the wounded, but in a few days that would change.

On July 29, 1967 an explosion occurred aboard the USS *Forrestal* at 1050. They were preparing for a second bombing strike on Hanoi that morning when a 5.0 inch (127.0 mm) Mk-32 "Zuni" rocket mounted on an F-4B Phantom accidentally fired. This caused a cascade of events that would impact me directly.

A call came over the PA system.

"Those that are off duty, grades E2 to E5, report to the geedunk area on C deck for a briefing by the XO."

I joined my shipmates as we sat on the deck. Scuttlebutt had circled the ship about the explosion on the *Forrestal*. The XO, or executive officer, stood in front of us, waiting until the stream of men entering the area slowed before speaking.

"Men, the captain feels we need to apprise you of the situation over on the USS *Forrestal* . You will all, ship's company and hospital, soon be involved. Here are the details of the event as we know them." He paused long enough for that to sink in before starting his briefing.

"A number of aircraft were preparing to launch when a rocket from a waiting Phantom lit up and fired. At this point we don't know why. The rocket flew across the flight deck, striking a wing-mounted external fuel tank on a Sky Hawk, also awaiting launch. The impact tore the tank off the wing and ignited the resulting spray of escaping JP fuel. This caused an instantaneous conflagration. We know that more fuel tanks on the Sky Hawk overheated and ruptured, releasing more jet fuel, which increased the flames. This burning fuel then spread along the flight deck."

The XO turned to a master chief standing by him. "Chief, take over for me. I need to return to the Com room." He exited quickly as the chief began speaking.

"Multiple bombs and rockets were cooked off by the fire. The *Forrestal* is burning and taking massive casualties. You will all be getting assignments to respond to the situation shortly. Report to your duty stations and wait for further orders."

I hurried to my ward on A level. "Lara, you report to the meeting area on C deck immediately," said Lt. Hildebrand, the duty nurse on my ward. "You're going to join the response team. I just got the order for you." She turned to speak to another corpsman as I left.

It was 2100, and I was off duty so I was assigned to the special teams being put together.

Thirty-five corpsmen and twenty ship's crew gathered again at the geedunk space, located in the middle of a boulevard passageway that went directly through the ship, stem to stern. It was located on C deck, the middle deck and the widest part of the ship. In front of the geedunk store was a large space that was often used for teams of crewmembers getting special assignment orders.

"Men," said an officer, standing next to the head nurse, "I just got off the horn with HM2 Paul Streetman. His team of thirty-seven corpsmen has been dealing with casualties and is stretched to the point of collapse. Basically his staff is overwhelmed. We will send over a small group of corpsmen to give a hand once we reach them. I suspect that will occur at approximately 0230." The officer had been getting detailed reports and continued. "The USS *Forrestal* is being escorted by the USS *Henry W. Tucker*, a destroyer, and is steaming toward us now. We've been underway too, and will meet them near the Tonkin Gulf. This will allow the crew to begin transferring the dead and wounded to us beginning at 0400.

"Once we start taking on the wounded and dead, we will shut down the ship to all crew and patients. The only people allowed in passageways and outside decks will be you men standing here. Petty Officer Kerr?" A sailor I'd noticed before on the ship, the commissary storekeeper, stepped forward. "Take half our men here below and clear out number one and two cold storage lockers. I need them empty. Don't concern yourself with spoilage. Understand?"

Kerr nodded and took ten of the ship's crew below.

"The rest of you men, peel off and join me forward near the main elevator." He and the rest of the ship's crew left, leaving us corpsmen with our head nurse, Lt. Commander Kovasovich.

"Listen up, corpsmen," she said. "The *Forrestal* has indicated that most of the injured have been evacuated to the *Enterprise* and *Oriskany* aircraft carriers, and will be underway shortly to the naval hospital at Yokosuka. They can make better speed and the less seriously burned and injured can be stabilized aboard those ships' medical facilities long enough to make it to Japan. I suspect we will get perhaps less than thirty injured, but these will be the most critically wounded and will be taken to OR and ICU immediately, so you men here," she held her arms out and separated about half the corpsmen, "will take on those responsibilities. Split off now and report to Lt. Wong in the triage area. She'll divide half of you to flight quarters station." The guys left quickly. "Ten of you report to Lt. Durbin on the flight deck. You'll be going over to the *Forrestal* to assist in transferring the injured and dead." She indicated nine others and me. KC, Don, and Bobby were also part of this team.

As we left, she continued to voice orders to the remaining medical staff on various jobs that were anticipated. I thought I knew what was coming. I'd seen a lot already. I had been there nine months; burns were the same, whether from bombs, napalm, or diesel fuel in a burn pit. Or at least that was what I thought.

"My brothers need me. My brothers need me. My brothers need me," I repeated in my head as I boarded a chopper sent by the *Forrestal* to take us to the burning ship.

It was still smoldering, though no flames showed, but even in the dark I could make out a black cloud rising above the carrier. I remembered the newsreels of World War II. The black and white images of that era played out in the movie of my life. But in real life I could see tangible smoke, it had substance, thickness, and weight as it rose into the sky. Soon I would smell it. Kerosene and naphtha with some gasoline mixed in, plus diesel and maybe napalm. A real witch's brew of chemicals. The smell would stay with me the rest of my life.

We'd lit up our ship, which had been darkened for the journey into enemy waters, the Gulf of Tonkin. A radio call went out to the North Vietnamese that we, the *Repose*, were on a mercy mission and that we requested that the "UN Convention of Medical Mercy Missions" be invoked to protect us from attack by their gunships. Silently, we all prayed they honored that request.

As we landed on the carrier, HM2 Streetman met us for a brief meeting. "The wounded are already heading to the *Repose*. I need your help with the dead. We've bagged most of them, but we still have twenty-plus missing. Help us find them and then bag them for transport," he said, as alarms and orders screamed from the PA overhead.

It was controlled pandemonium. All officers, as far I could see, and men were doing what needed to be done with no matter of rank. Side by side, they worked like dogs in a sled team, SOS'ing their asses off.

I walked through the dark passages toward crew quarters that had been directly under the exploding planes and bombs. We had no power, only red and bright white battery-powered emergency lanterns to guide us. Water had pooled to about a foot deep from the fire suppression laid down by the crew. Soot from the fires coated the surface of these watery passages. I felt like I was walking on black clouds because of the surreal nature of oil and chemicals mixing with water.

Entering the burnt out crew area under the flight deck, I was struck by the sight of what became a flaming tomb for sailors aboard the *Forrestal*. It was a twisted mass of steel girders, all seared with the heat of burning fuel, a macabre scene of piled metal with no resemblance to crew's quarters found on Navy ships.

Bobby pointed to our left. "Can't get into that area, just too much twisted metal. But straight ahead, I think those are bunks stacked on each other. Let's lift that stuff off and check each layer."

I flashed on a memory of charcoal sketch done by sailors in World War II. It was dark and confusing imagery, like that we were facing. I located a man or what was left of him. He'd been in his rack when burning fuel poured onto him. He'd had no time to react so he was probably sleeping at the time. His arm covered his eyes, like how I slept sometimes in my own bunk. I notified Petty Officer Streetman.

"Where can I get more body bags? Our team has run out of them, and we still have five more bodies to bag," I said.

"Go see the ship's sailmaker and ask him if he can quick-stitch some canvas together for you to use. I know we're out. There's none anywhere on the ship that I know of. Besides, you guys need to get back to the *Repose* and do what I do not want to do myself." He indicated where I needed to go to find the sailmaker.

As I made my way through dark passages, the ghosts of those that had just died seemed to lurk in the shadows. I was spooked and turned my thoughts to the mundane. I wondered why they had the rank of a ship's sailmaker on a modern ship. Sails had disappeared a century ago. It was the only way to keep myself self from sinking emotionally into the horror around me.

I returned to the *Repose* with about twenty dead bodies piled three high in the back of a Chinook chopper, stacked like a cord of wood. In the end the *Repose* took a hundred and twenty six bodies. My Hospital Auxiliary Ship was now being turned into a morgue. I didn't return to the *Forrestal* for more bodies, instead I was assigned graves duty.

As we unloaded the dead onto our ship, an unreal atmosphere surrounded us. No one was in sight except for the minimum crew necessary for the landing choppers. The gangways, passages and decks were empty. It was o-dark-thirty, but on our ship there were always people moving about at that hour. Not tonight. No one moved except those men who had first met in the geedunk area at the beginning of this nightmare.

We removed the body bags first by stretcher and then by grabbing the end of bags and dragging them down empty corridors. We took them to the cold storage lockers that had been emptied by Kerr and his men.

Some of the crew and corpsmen who had not been to the *Forrestal* were scurrying around as we unloaded body bag after body bag. They were clean-up teams, tasked with wiping up blood and body fluids that leaked from the dead in the aptly named bags. They were not waterproof.

"Bobby, this one is draining blood and pus. I need to lift my end higher. You got a grip?" I asked as we carried a body bag down the ladders to the hold area, six decks below the flight deck, where the cold storage lockers were located. The bag leaked clear, smelly liquids, maybe plasma.

Sometimes the elevator was available, and we took several bags at once. We crowded them in with more than the maximum persons allowed, shut the door and sent them alone. At the bottom, waiting men carried them to the refrigerators. But when the elevator was in use, we humped down the ship's ladders.

"Get this goddamn job done ASAP," a chief yelled at one point, not with rancor, but with the need for speed. People were behind bulkheads, speculating on what was happening inches from them in passageways of The Angel of The Orient.

The clean-up teams were kept busy by the mess created as we dragged the dead through the empty halls and ladders of the ship. It stunk, and it was septic. The smell of disinfectant and the sound of rattling buckets followed our every step.

I was pulled into Cold Locker 1 and stood looking at the highest-ranking corpsman aboard, Chief Brody. "We need to get IDs on as many of these men as we can," he said. "They're beginning to rot, and if we don't do this now these men will never make it home. We don't need any more in the Tomb of the Unknown."

A cigar, wet and smelly, stuck out of his mouth. I suddenly wished I liked cigars. The smells coming from the bodies were becoming intolerable. I realized he was using the cigar to mask the odors.

The burned bodies were frozen in grotesque positions, like the sleeping sailor I had retrieved. The pilots, lying on their sides in the bags, were in sitting positions as if still seated in their cockpits. The damage control team that was first caught by the flames looked like alligators with their arms outstretched as they tried to crawl away from the flames that had caught them and burned them beyond recognition.

I had the bizarre notion at first that there must have been a lot of black guys aboard the ship. Wrong. They were charred black. It was stupid of me, but a sign that my brain had trouble comprehending the horror of the sight. The completely burned bodies did not horrify me as much as the partially burned men. Their bodies were beginning to grow germs in intestines, stomachs, and other organs that were only partially cooked, bacteria like escherichia coli, shigella, and the multitude of different salmonellas found in our gut. This made the intestines and stomach balloon and bloom into multicolored shades that made my anatomy books come alive. My stomach churned.

Some of these balloons exploded, releasing gases that permeated everything in the room. The smells of the bacteria, sickeningly sweet but putrid, filled the air. The smell of death.

I turned to Kerr, the store's guy. "Can you open up the hatch there and let in some air?"

A hatch was built into the side of the ship that allowed for easy transfer of foodstuffs while replenishing supplies. He unlatched it and swung it open, exposing the sea rolling by in beautiful blue waves about twelve feet below. The air was fresh and cool. I stood watching it for a moment, the beauty of the rolling waves, my hair blowing as if I were aboard a luxury yacht.

The worst part came as the chief in charge told me to get as many scalpels, chest spreaders, and any instrument that could be used as a crowbar that I could grab from the OR. I walked down the passageway and up one deck where Tom worked. He was my go-to man for stuff like this. I told him what I needed.

"Do they have to be sterile?" Tom asked with a worried look as he studied my face. I wondered what it showed.

"Sterile is no concern down where the dead are. Give me everything you got, sterile or not."

He piled a bunch of instruments in a couple of square metal pans. The sound of metal banging on metal echoed off the hull in the area he worked in. Tom added some large chest spreaders in trays and followed me down to the dead zone.

I handed the chief one of the trays. "Here you go," I said.

He placed it atop a wood plank that had been set on a couple of oil drum-sized barrels in the middle of the locker. Tom and I put the rest on the plank.

"All right, listen up!" Fifteen corpsmen and a half dozen ship's crew turned to the chief. "Here's the deal. We will collect as much identifying material from these men as possible, clothing with stenciled names, dog tags, any liberty cards found in pockets. Anything with a name on it. Body bags will be numbered and tags that correspond to those numbers will be put on the ankles or legs of these guys. I'll have envelopes also numbered. They'll be in numerical order and anything you find put it in these envelopes. Make sure the body's number is the same as the envelope's number."

He held up the scalpels. "These are to be used to cut the face from ear to mouth edge, and," he displayed a surgical chest spreader, "these to break open the jaws. Each of you partner up in pairs. I have clipboards with blank teeth charts. Get down and diagram every man's mouth on the chart. Put the tag number on the chart and stick that in the envelope, too." We all froze for a moment. Seeing the horror in our eyes, the chief stopped for a moment and caught his breath before speaking again. This time his strident tone was almost a whisper. "Teeth are the only foolproof way of identification. We have to get them home to their families. I know what we're asking here is a lot, but it's got to be done, for the families." He choked up. Tears pooled in his eyes before he quietly commanded, "Get to work."

Not a word more was said by anyone in the detail. Later, I did not talk to Tom or anyone else about what had happened. Not even to Bobby or Kerr. What we had witnessed, what we had done, was literally unspeakable. We just couldn't put it into words.

We got underway for Singapore on August 3, 1967, arriving on August 7 for five days of liberty.

Chapter Twelve

The Group in Singapore

O n August 6, 1967, the *Repose* crossed the equator on our way to Singapore at 105 degrees longitude, 25 degrees E latitude. Navy tradition dictated that a sailor undertake an initiation ritual if he had never crossed the equator at sea. Sailors who had not been initiated are called "pollywogs," and I was one of them, as was most of the medical staff aboard. The crossing was arranged by sailing past our destination, Singapore, by some miles because it was a privilege to become a "shellback," those who had performed the ritual. Today the ritual is more of a hazing rite done for morale purposes, but in the past it was a loyalty test.

The night before the scheduled crossing, the pollywogs, or wogs for short, revolt and capture old shellback seamen. Then mock courts are set up and charges brought against the wogs. The following day we are punished. A charming day is spent on deck kissing the belly of King Neptune, which has been smeared with cooking grease from the galley, followed by a series of ever more humiliating activities.

It turned out to be the most fun day of my time aboard the *Repose*. I was proud and honored to be put in that special sailor "The Order of the Shellbacks." The initiation also served to take my mind off the events that had transpired on the *Forrestal*. By the time I reached Singapore, I was raring to have some fun.

I received a shortwave telegram message from Matt saying that he and Joe would fly into Singapore with a couple of Marines on August 9 on a three-night pass. One of the men was British, an observer with the 9th Marine Regiment. In the message, he included the fact that the gentlemen were part of The Group.

We pulled into HMS Terror on August 7 near noon. In keeping with the Royal Navy's tradition of naming their naval bases and dockyards after ships, the base was named after an Erebus-class monitor ship, which was based at one time in Singapore before World War II. It had performed distinguished service in line with colonization activity. The British took official control of this island state in 1945.

I asked a British sailor dockside what the difference was between HMS *Terror* the ship and HMS Terror the base. "The ship is Her Majesty's Ship, while the base is Her Majesty's Service," he said.

That was easy to figure out, I thought, as I walked away still confused.

Docked next to us was a British heavy-navy repair ship, the HMS *Triumph* (A108). It had been arranged that our crew, both officers and enlisted, would have dinner aboard her the first night in port as guests of the Royal Navy.

Since it was a troop transport as well as a repair ship, the ship had facilities for both crews to take part. I found a British medical corpsman to sit with, and we spent a fantastic evening swapping sea stories.

"I see your insignia has the caduceus snake and staff like ours, but what's on top?" I had spotted the patch on his dress whites, and while it resembled ours, his had a knob on top.

"That's the sovereign's crown. See?" He lifted his sleeve and showed me a beautiful tattoo on his shoulder that showed the snake and staff topped with a fancy royal crown. I spotted Bobby watching me down the way and gave him a nod toward the sailor hiking his sleeve. He smiled with a knowing look as to what I was indicating.

After dinner, Tom and Bobby joined me dockside to grab a cab into Singapore.

"You want us to get tattoos, right?" Bobby asked.

"Bingo," I said. "With 'The Group' tattooed underneath the caduceus."

He laughed while I explained to Tom what we were talking about. He loved the idea.

"Let's wait til Matt and Joe get here, and we'll all get one at the same time," he said.

We shook on it as the three of us went into town to have a Singapore sling at the bar in the Raffles Hotel, where the lovely concoction was invented. The Long Bar had been patronized over the decades by a host of literati, including Ernest Hemingway and Somerset Maugham. So the drink traveled around the world and with a name that always seemed exotic and sophisticated. What better place than the bar where it was invented to have one?

We pulled into the hotel's main entrance and headed for the bar. The Raffles had English, colonial-style architecture, very fancy in that British way. Two Armenian brothers from Persia, Martin and Tigran Sarkies, established it in 1887. In later years they were joined by younger brothers Aviet and Arshak and kinsman Martyrose Arathoon. With their innovative cuisine and extensive detail to British colonial attitude, the firm built the hotel into Singapore's best-known icon. It was named after Stamford Raffles, the founder of modern Singapore, whose statue had stood in the main courtyard of this elegant establishment since 1887.

We sat in the bar drinking very disappointing Singapore slings. As it turns out, they did not use the sweet sloe gin that we used in the States. It tasted nothing like it had been described to me. We quickly changed our cocktails of choice.

"I got an idea," Bobby said. "Let's pool our money and rent a suite for tomorrow night. Then when the guys get here on Wednesday, we'll have a big dinner here at the hotel for the entire Group."

Tom and I agreed immediately, and we headed to the front desk and made a reservation for the one night at a cost of $48, which was all we could afford. We also ordered for dinner for the seven of us the following evening.

"Where would you like the meal served, gentlemen?" asked the desk clerk in a crisp British accent.

We looked at each other and simultaneously asked, "Where may we have it served?" Unconsciously, we imitated his inflection, which made us sound like we were mocking him.

The clerk called over a bellboy and explained that we could have it anywhere we wanted. The bellboy would take us on a quick tour. A central court was located in the hotel just off the Long Bar's exterior entrance. It was there that we asked for our table. The area was grassy and had tropical fan palms scattered randomly among fountains and walkways with strategically placed flowerbeds. The weather was warm and balmy, and the forecast held the promise of the same for the remainder of our stay.

We returned to the ship for the night. The next day I left a note with the OD (officer of the day) telling Matt where to meet us. He had made that logistics suggestion in his telegram, what was known as a MARS gram in the Navy.

After checking into the hotel, we went shopping and sightseeing in Singapore, then returned to wait for Matt and Joe. The room at the Raffles was the most marvelous thing we sailors had experienced, the beds especially. They were soft and plush, which definitely beat sleeping on canvas sailcloth on a swaying ship.

The three of us talked and drank room-service cocktails, luxuriating as we waited for the rest of The Group. The phone rang close to 11 a.m. It was the concierge.

"Your guests have arrived. Mr. Horn and party are waiting on the veranda."

We scrambled downstairs. As we approached them, Matt stood, as did Joe and two strapping Marines, one British and one American.

"Gentlemen, may I introduce Corporal David Bassett of the Royal Marines and Corporal Bob LeBlanc," Matt said.

We were all wearing our dress uniforms, and the seven of us made quite a dashing group. We sat and ordered drinks. Cpl. Bassett took over.

"I have an automobile at my disposal, a Safari Land Rover, that will accommodate us all. I also made reservations at the Royal Asiatic Society Club not far from here. I thought we'd take tea there and maybe luncheon, as well."

I almost swooned. Man, was he handsome. On the way to the club, Bassett spoke to us about protocol. "The club is whites only. No Asians, Indians, Chinese, mixed race or Negroes are allowed. Use a soft voice as we talk and follow my actions on drinking tea and eating."

He smiled charmingly, unaware how he sounded to revolutionary Americans. My eyes opened to British thinking on race and general prejudice in the world. It wasn't really much different from the American attitudes concerning blacks and Mexicans back home, I thought. We had tea and sandwiches for lunch and I learned a lot about colonial society.

That evening we had our dinner in the courtyard of the Raffles as arranged. For me, that meant steak. We got to know each other quickly and at one point talked about our careers in the military.

I asked LeBlanc if he'd been in Dong Ha.

He nodded. "I'm almost finished. I'll return stateside in two months. But I've requested a second deployment. I'm coming back next March."

"Gung ho!" I said.

He nodded again with no embarrassment, which indicated he was dedicated to the corps and to the war. I asked how his being gay squared with that. But like me he felt the military was separate from our reality, and that he would work within the system to survive.

I announced that I'd applied for laboratory technician school, and had already received orders for San Diego Naval Hospital for training when I finished my tour in two months.

This prompted responses from Bobby, Tom, and Joe. They wanted to stay together and had all requested orders for any duty around Washington, D.C. I suspected they would all end up at Bethesda Naval Hospital in Maryland and said as much.

"That would be great," Bobby said. He radiated happiness, and it translated to the rest of us.

Matt's face showed pain but also what I thought was resolve or determination. Then he spoke.

"Does it seem odd to you guys that we soldiers never think about our own mortality? Freud tells us our unconscious is inaccessible to the conception of our own death, that we are inclined to kill the stranger, as was primitive man, but never think about our own death."

"So you're saying we're all cavemen when it comes to our conventionally civilized attitude toward death? And it's war that shows us our disconnection with it, even as we kill?" asked our British Marine, Bassett.

"Yes," continued Matt. "War forces us to be heroes who cannot believe in their own demise, and it tells us to rise above the death of those we love, our fellow soldiers. But we never think about dying ourselves."

It wasn't a downer that Matt had started this conversation. In the back of my mind, I was thinking about the remaining months of my duty in Vietnam, even as the boys were talking about future duty stations. I was worried about making it to the finish line, too. Matt was voicing my thoughts and probably those on all our minds. He suddenly brightened.

"But I forgot that nature in me because I've re-upped."

The six of us stared at him. My mind raced. Did he mean in the service?

"I've extended my duty here in Nam. I will stay with Charlie One Nine for four more months and won't be going stateside next month after all. I had orders but I changed them just before we left the Nam to come and meet you guys."

"Hey, hey, hey, Audie Murphy!" LeBlanc shouted, using the term we'd adopted for the man who stepped into harm's way. This was in reference to the highly decorated Audie L. Murphy of WWII, who later became an actor.

While the others laughed and slapped Matt on the back, I grew fearful, and I realized I loved him. I found I could not rise above the prospect of his death, of losing him. As we sat next to the statue of Stamford Raffles, a frightened feeling came over me. I couldn't shake it for the rest of dinner.

When we finished, the others went inside while Matt and I lingered in the courtyard. "Let me get us a drink. What do you want?" Matt asked.

"Can we just talk?"

He nodded. He knew what this was about. "I meant to talk with you before telling the others about re-upping. I'm sorry, babe. I know we wanted to see each other stateside."

"Well then, why?" I said, almost whining. I wanted to cry but I held my emotion in check. I'd learned to do that because of all the tragedy around me; it was the only way I could do my job. "I know how you feel about this war, the same as I do. There's no point to it. Like you said the first day I met you, we're winning the losing battle, and after a year I know that to be true." My voice became louder as my anger rose. "Why the fuck are you doing this? We've made it. Why prove you're the biggest caveman? I'm scared and pissed. Really, what the fuck?"

He grabbed me, pulling me into his chest, trying to steady my trembling body. "Don't, baby, don't. I need to do this. Most of the men in the unit I've been with are staying on. Please don't hate me. I can't leave and you know it. It's something I cannot do, even for you." Matt kissed me, and I quieted down.

"I know you have to. We're like a pack of dogs. You do what the pack does, right or wrong. I know that's true. I'm used to thinking that way. It allows me to be here doing the job of corpsman. I want to be an anti-war hippie. I really do. But that's not in me," I said. "I do this for the men I help. Without judging the war, I push through. But I wish for so much, and my wishes have you in them."

With no more to say, we kissed again. He'd already extended his tour, and the military doesn't allow you to un-volunteer.

We went inside and joined the others. I tucked away my thoughts as I've always done. The military and war demands that.

Our night ended. Matt, Ski, and their two friends went to stay in transit barracks at the base. The base saw a lot of R&R servicemen so services and accommodations were available free to all military in operation in Vietnam.

The next morning Tom, Bobby and I checked out of the Raffles and returned to HMS Terror and boarded our ship. Matt came over and grabbed us all to hang out with him and Ski, plus the guys. I put my arm around Matt's neck as we left the ship. Walking down the plank, we filed off one by one to our waiting companions on shore.

"I'm glad to see you two are okay this morning," Bobby whispered to my back. I guessed the rest of The Group had sensed our mood the night before. They knew what it was about, and I felt their support without exchanging a word.

"All right, mates. We have one night to do the town before Matt, Joe, LeBlanc and I go back into action so I've planned a special evening," announced our butch British Marine. "At midnight tonight we attempt the Dance of the Flaming Arsehole!"

"What the fuck is he talking about?" Tom asked to no one in particular.

I chimed in that I was working with plenty of them already.

"Tonight we go to Boogie Street," Cpl. Bassett said. "And my friends, you have never experienced anything like this."

Boogie Street was actually Bugis Street, which was located in the heart of the city-state of Singapore. Sailors and Marines had morphed the name into something that reflected the true nature of the thoroughfare. It was renowned internationally for a nightly gathering of men in drag. It had become such a phenomenon that Boogie Street was one of Singapore's top destinations for military men on leave.

After a day of shopping and hanging out at the British EM Club, we started our journey to Boogie Street and Bassett filled us in on the history of the place.

"These queens began to rendezvous in the area in the 1950s, which of course started to attract Westerners who came for the booze, the food, the pasar malam shopping and of course the girls. Boogie Street has become really popular now that war has come to Asia. It is so renowned that there is a nightly parade of crazy transvestites walking up and down the street. Some even have gone the whole Christine Jorgensen route, and are now 'real women.' Caucasian gawkers come every night. These Asian and Eurasian queens like to tease and torment men in uniform; they sit on your lap to pose for photographs. But watch it! They charge money for the privilege, and it's not cheap.

"Some sashay about looking to hook drunken sailors and GIs on R&R for an hour of profitable intimacy." Bassett arched his eyebrows. "I think drunk straight guys get a thrill out of sex with an exotic Oriental. None of them will ever admit it but the added spice of crossing the gender boundary in a sleazy hovel appeals to their latent homosexuality."

Bobby piped up. "That's not a problem for any of us in The Group. That's for sure. I prefer my men with beards. You can keep the ladyboys for the suppressed straight guys."

"There's a saying among Westerners that one can easily tell who's a real female. Those that are drop-dead gorgeous are transvestites. The rest? Well, they're real women," Bassett added.

That got us laughing as we pulled up to Boogie Street for a night of high adventure. The amount of revenue that the queens of Bugis Street raked in was considerable, providing a huge booster shot of money for Singapore so the government looked the other way. The notorious section began at Victoria Street West and ended at Queen Street.

As The Group walked about, we reached an area halfway between the two roadways where the ladies had set up an open-air nightclub. Tables and chairs were pulled into the middle of the street that was closed to traffic at midnight. Each table had nice tablecloths and candles, which softened the harsh jaw line of men posing as women. There was also a well-patronized public toilet with a flat roof.

While The Group sat among the "gurrls" of Boogie Street for a couple of drinks, it was the flaming arse that we really wanted to see. Our British Marine gathered us up and we staggered down to the intersection of Victoria and Queen.

"You said they put a burning newspaper up their butts? Why?" I asked our British guide.

He laughed. "It's to see how long they can last before they pull it out. But really, it's cause they're crazy fuckin Brits who like to burn newspapers stuck up their bums. Here we are, the gents." He halted in front of a men's restroom. "I see we're fortunate tonight. We have an arse ready and waiting." He extended an arm like a ringmaster in a circus to the roof of the men's toilet.

As he waved his hand, the ritual began. The newspaper had been inserted into the ass of a swabbie and lit. The English sailor danced and bucked back and forth while bent over so as not to catch his jumper on fire. His movement was made all the more awkward because his pants and underwear hung around his ankles.

His compatriots gathered around, chanting, "Haul 'em down, you Zulu warrior, Haul 'em down, you Zulu warrior. Haul 'em down, you Zulu chief chief chief. Allelele zumba zumba zumba hey!"

The Group, including myself, was drunk so we clapped and sang along with the burning arse's mates. Everyone was arm and arm. I took this opportunity to hold Matt in a way that I hoped would show my real feelings toward him. He stood in front of me singing loudly, he in his Marine khakis and me in dress whites. I wrapped my arms around him, and he leaned back into my chest, letting his head loll against my shoulder. He took my hands in his and we sang together.

"That has got to be the hairiest, lowest-hanging pair of balls I have ever seen," he said with a laugh.

The moment was so much fun, a release after everything we'd been through. He looked up at me with glistening eyes that said he wanted to kiss me. But fear of discovery haunted us, so we avoided the temptation of showing our love. It was hard. I so wanted to kiss his beautiful mouth again.

There were a few other men from our ship on Boogie Street. The psych that had treated my man-overboard patient was there with a very handsome Australian officer. I didn't know if he was gay. Most of the men on Boogie Street were not. I smiled at him and he smiled back with a knowing nod.

"Hey, looky over there," said Tom, chinpointing across the street. "It's Bubbles and Squawk."

They were a known "couple" on the *Repose*. No one bothered them or cared that they were lovers. They were very sweet guys and harmless to the masculine ethos aboard a naval ship.

"They're a cute couple. David, take me over and introduce me, I love meeting other gays in the service," Matt pleaded.

We sauntered over, stopping on the way to grab some beers for us and them.

After introducing Matt to Bubbles and Squawk, he asked, "Why do they call you Bubbles and Squawk?"

"It's because I work on the ship's water evaporator system that converts seawater to drinkable H2O. That means I'm boiling water all day and so the name, Bubbles," he explained. "My honey here, Squawk, is just a deck ape, but he stands relief duty as a radio guy. In fact he does most of the MARS calls on the ship."

"So, are you two lovers?" Squawk asked, with his arm around Bubbles and smiling with a touch of nasty to it.

"We haven't had a chance." Matt and I answered in unison, which busted us all up with laughter.

As we headed back to The Group, Matt turned to me. "I wish I could be your lover. I really like you. I wish we could have something together."

I didn't have a chance to answer as we rejoined the gang.

"You guys look cute together, and I hate to break this up. But we gotta get back. It's late," Tom said.

As we headed back to the car, I spotted David Monarch, the black corpsman aboard our ship. He was making out with an Australian sailor in an alley off Boogie Street. I pointed him out to Matt.

"I can't help but think critically of him for doing such a thing in public. Why would someone do such a stupid thing with all that's at stake if caught?" I said.

Matt smirked. "It's not the flavor he likes. It's the crunch." His pithy comment said it all.

I soon forgot about David Monarch as memory of the flaming arse had us singing "Zulu warrior" back to the car. We were very drunk, and Matt, who was the most sober one, had to drive back to base. In the backseat were our British Marine, Tom, and LeBlanc. Bobby and I were in the front seat with Matt. Joe was in the very back of the Land Rover, passed out.

"Three queers in the back seat, which one will the Marine choose? Which one will have the nice one?" sang Bobby, drunkenly making up lyrics from the soundtrack of a popular movie, "Three Coins in a Fountain." In their drunken state, he and British Marine were making out with each other.

The Group was also sporting new tattoos. We all got cut together that night on Boogie Street: a caduceus with the words THE GROUP under it in a crescent that pointed upward.

We sailed back to Vietnam on August 12. As we pulled away, Matt, Joe, and the two Marines waved goodbye from the dock. Their plane was due for takeoff in a few hours. I would see them one more time.

My orders were to leave the ship in October. I would spend a week at Dong Ha before I di-di'ed back to the good old USA, or "the world" as we had come to call it.

The *Repose* spent the next four weeks on station, taking on wounded from Da Nang to Dong Ha and all points between. On September 13, the USS *Repose* weighed anchor for Subic Bay and my last liberty in Olongapo City.

CHAPTER THIRTEEN

Con Thien

The *Repose* spent only a few days in Subic that early September. While in port, I said goodbye to my bar girl, Vangie. She had given me good cover. I never asked nor received sexual favors from her. I knew she was happy to have respite from a manhandling sailor. She still got money from me, so charity it wasn't. But we had an understanding.

I also had breakfast at my favorite Quonset hut in another ritualistic goodbye. A Denver omelet never tasted as good as those in Subic. I doubted I would ever see this part of the globe again, and I wanted to remember it.

Tom, Bobby, and I hung out together the entire time while in port. "Let's hit all our haunts, Grande Island, Cubi Point, and the China Seas EM Club," I said as we ambled down the gangway of the *Repose*.

In the China Seas Club we flicked cigarette ashes into our pitchers of beer, legend had it that it helped to get us drunk faster. Drinking to inebriation had become the favorite pastime for the entire crew, especially the corpsmen. The daily sight of bleeding Marines and the moans of the wounded were always present in our heads. Drunken nights in Olongapo City were routine now. It shut out everything we'd been through, but only for a little while.

Just before midnight, my Group and I joined hundreds of soused sailors who came running and stumbling down the main drag of Olongapo to cross the bridge that led to the main gate. This was curfew for enlisted men below a certain rank. It was a bizarre ritual that I thoroughly enjoyed on our final night.

Our last day in Subic, The Group stood on deck, watching stores being brought aboard. We had ditched duty to watch the crew and corpsmen staying on after us hump aboard horse-cock, large square cans of sterilized milk, and other provisions.

Tom pointed down the dock. Three Naval MPs and a Marine officer were marching a black sailor between them. As they got closer, I recognized the sailor.

"It's Monarch. David Monarch." He was being escorted, which meant he was under arrest.

The rumors flowed below decks like bilge water. KC joined us topside, bringing the latest.

"He got caught with a guy last night doing the nasty." KC had a disappointed look on his face. "It's not the news that he's gay that hurts me. It's that he's my shipmate, and now his entire life is going to be ruined." No matter what KC thought of David's gayness, Monarch was still one of us. Sadness seemed to fill the whole ship.

Unspoken words flew between Tom, Bobby, and myself in the form of exchanged looks. We had to be extra careful now. The witch-hunt would start, although I suspected it would end the moment we set sail.

I had a profound sense of shame when I encountered David in the crew's quarters as he packed his sea bag. Two MPs stood over him. We made quick eye contact, and then I looked away, shunning him. I didn't say a word, not goodbye, not I'm sorry, nothing.

I felt sick to my stomach at my cowardice.

We learned later that the "nasty" thing Monarch was caught doing was making out with a white Marine, which in the U.S. of A. in the 1960s was the most egregious thing a black man could do. Monarch's court-martial sentenced him to nineteen months in prison at Leavenworth, Kansas. At the end of his sentence, a dishonorable discharge would greet him, and the loss of all military benefits. All for being a gay black man who had the temerity to kiss a white man while at war.

On September 20 the *Repose* returned to duty off the coast of Vietnam. Once we arrived I was ordered to leave for the aid station at Dong Ha. A sweep of the DMZ was in full swing—Operation Kingfisher, a multi-taskforce military action. Casualties were high. They needed more corpsmen at Dong Ha. KC, Don, and I were part of the backfill team ordered up.

The Group stood on the deck just off triage.

"Tom, Bobby, I hate to make this a movie ending, but this is it," I said. "I won't see you again. My orders are for in-country until my return to the world. I finish my tour on the ground."

Bobby cried and Tom stood stoic. I cried, too, and hugged them both hard, with my arms wrapped around them. I wished with all my heart that this wasn't happening.

"I didn't expect it to end this way," Tom said. "After all the shit we've been through, I was looking forward to going home together."

"Me, too. You guys write and let me know where you end up. Maybe someday The Group will get together. Who knows?"

I was imitating every bad war movie line I had ever heard. I may as well have said, "Meet me under the old rail station clock on New Year's Eve." But movies were the only model I had for an event like this.

Our head nurse arrived and said her goodbyes then we headed to the waiting Huey.

Badly wounded Marines had to be taken off the Huey and into triage before we could board. Tom ran to OR. Heartbroken or not, duty called. Bobby remained on deck. As we lifted off, I could see him standing at the rail, his body shaking from crying so hard. The chopper banked and headed to shore. The white pearl on the sea soon disappeared from view.

When I arrived, Matt stood on the helipad, a compacted dirt landing space that allowed for about twenty choppers of various sizes. It was located a short distance from the "cheese grater" metal landing field used by heavier planes, even those as big as the Star Lifter that brought me to Vietnam.

Over the roar of landing Hueys and Chinooks, I climbed down and Matt took my sea bag.

"What the hell's up? What's the urgency?" I yelled.

"Let's get to the hooch. I'm off duty now and we can talk."

We ducked and ran to a Jeep and headed toward the aid station I'd become familiar with. Once inside our tent, he clued me in.

"The NVA have artillery, mobile, on the north side of the DMZ. Because it's movable, our counter-battery can't take them out. That shit even has enough range that we get incoming here at Dong Ha some nights. But right now the north is pounding Con Thien like a motherfucker."

"I heard 3rd Battalion is covering the position now. Go on," I replied.

"The NVA has started a major shelling campaign on the Meat Grinder." Matt used the term the Marines had given Con Thien. "They're getting howitzer shells, 120mm and 82mm mortars and a shitload of rockets daily. We've been unable to get in for three days now. We can't take out the wounded. Things are desperate. So we'll have a tough assignment as soon as command figures out how to get a fucking dust-off in there."

History would record that more than fourteen hundred Marines were killed and over nine thousand wounded in and around Con Thien.

Matt told me that Cpl. LeBlanc was there. They hadn't heard from him for several days. Joe entered, sporting that wild-eyed adrenaline look I'd seen that night when I met him almost a year ago. He'd just flown in from a pickup at another hot spot, Hill 889.

We spent the night shooting the shit. Around 0400, a batch of Marines shuffled near our tent. I popped my head out and saw eight men covered in bright red mud.

"You guys from Con Thien?" I asked them.

"We've just come off the citadel, drove through Charlie Country. We had to. That was the only way to get to an LZ that was clear of the rockets incoming from the DMZ."

Matt moved from behind me. "Any of you hurt? Why you covered in so much mud?" He switched into corpsman mode, surveying the men for signs of injury.

The Marines answered. "We're okay, Doc. The mud is because the NVA's throwing up so much hot metal with the rockets and mortars that you need to crawl on the ground to get anywhere. No chance to get up. The firing is so fucking mad. Plus it's been raining off and on for days now."

One of them knew Matt and addressed him directly. "There's a lot of wounded up there. Some pretty messed up guys. When's command getting those men out of there? It's been almost a week."

"We know. The weather and the shelling have made it impossible. I'm checking in with the CO tomorrow AM. I'll press him and see if we can find pilots to damn the danger and get us in. Check back with me around 0900," Matt said.

I worked shifts in the OR as I'd done before. Matt pulled duty that night with me.

"You do know we're going to have to volunteer to go in and get those guys," he half-asked.

"I know," I answered. "Set it up with the CO, and I'll go with you to get those men."

"It'll be dangerous as hell. But I know you already, David. I saw the character in you the first time we met." We stood next to my equipment sterilization area in the courtyard. He took my hands in his. "Why haven't we made love?"

I laughed. "We haven't had a goddamn chance, remember?"

"But you want to, don't you?" he asked me.

I nodded and leaned in to kiss him lightly on the lips. I quickly pulled back. "After that time in Hong Kong, I've been so afraid of getting caught. I know your career in the Marines is paramount in your life. I won't do anything to jeopardize that in any way. It's weird how we only live half a life because of the ignorant bigotry that surrounds us."

"I know, but I'll be getting back to the world eventually, I promise. The first place I am heading is to you in San Diego."

"And your parents?" I asked.

"They can wait. I want us to get to know each other. I want us to run away to a hotel on the beach for a few days and just be us, you and me, two guys who just happen to love each other." Throwing caution to the wind, we took a longer passionate kiss than the first peck I'd given him.

On my fourth day after leaving the ship, word came down that we were heading out. Matt, Joe, myself, and three other corpsmen reported to the officer in charge of the first attempt at getting a dust-off into Con Thien.

"There are three large hills that are connected, making up the base at Con Thien, the tallest is five hundred feet high," said the officer in charge of the scheme. "The procedure, men, will be to take three choppers up. The first two will land and pick up wounded, then lift off, followed by the third. We've done this a million times. We'll use the landing pad on the lowest of the hills because it has the most cover from incoming."

Matt and I were assigned to the first landing. I hoped we'd be in the same ship but we got split up. Joe would be in the third chopper that would hang back until ours lifted off. The remaining volunteer corpsmen were distributed evenly between the three ships.

As we landed, I jumped out and met Matt and the other corpsmen to divvy up the wounded lying around the pickup area. One field corpsman stood waiting to assist. We split the wounded evenly between the two choppers.

"The rest of the docs are off hustling more casualties. We need another dust-off ricky-tick," shouted the field corpsman above the roar of the Hueys.

Weight really affected the speed and fuel consumption on a Huey so balance and wounded distribution was important. Matt did a quick check of the situation.

"Give one of those amputees to Lara's chopper and put the other in mine. That'll be better for us to handle in case they go into arrest."

Matt had been doing this for over a year. He knew his shit and commanded the situation into a better pickup order. We nodded and got to work. I got four stretchers and a couple of ambulatory wounded onto my chopper with the help of Marines who came with the field doc, and turned around for a last look.

Boom! A rocket hit Matt's chopper and flames erupted. I saw him at the door doing what I had just done. He had his back to the explosion. I saw that he was okay. He spun and grabbed two wounded that he had just loaded and started to run away from the burning Huey. Suddenly, seconds after getting hit, the chopper exploded. Matt and the men in his arms were blown into the air, landing not far from me.

I ran to him…my friend, my dream.

When I reached him, I knew at once he was dying.

Marines rushed forward and picked up the two men Matt had just saved. They were still alive, but with secondary wounds from the explosion. LeBlanc was with them, but broke away and ran to Matt and me. I reached down and lifted Matt's head with both my hands.

He looked at me with pleading eyes. "I wish...I wish...," he muttered and then he stopped. His eyes were barely open.

"I know," I broke into sobs. "I wish we could have been lovers. I know, Matt!" I yelled. "I love you, man. I love you!"

LeBlanc stood over us, as other Marines gathered around. No one cared that two men could love each other. Not at that point. Not there.

Then Matt died.

He died, his eyes closing on their own.

I bent my head onto his chest and sobbed uncontrollably. The first time I ever really cried the entire year in Vietnam. I was nineteen years old and felt I'd lived a lifetime. As it turned out, a year in a war zone lasted a lifetime.

"David, come on. You gotta go, man," LeBlanc pleaded. "I'll take care of him. You gotta go!" He screamed, tears streaming down his grimy face. "The chopper has to lift off, and you need to take care of your men."

He pointed to the wounded and the chopper I came in on. Its rotor blades were spinning like mad. If it didn't lift off soon, it could get blown away, like Matt's. Rockets were blasting and bursting around us. LeBlanc grabbed my chin and forced me to look at him.

"You've been here long enough! You know how this works!" I stared at him, pain contorting my face. Then he whispered, "The friendship is over. Now go."

I frantically searched Matt's pockets. I knew he carried his Zippo inscribed with The Group everywhere with him, just like I did, like all of us did in The Group. I found the lighter. I wanted something of him, something to keep forever of this beautiful blond boy, only twenty-one years old, a short fucker and cute as hell.

All five of us were in Hong Kong, New Year's, 1966. We sailors, these five who'd raised hell getting tattoos, drinking too much, and having men. The adventures we had together were bound up in these Zippos. Bad boys, all of us, who smoked too many cigarettes, like Humphrey Bogart. We Zippo boys who had a secret that could land us in Leavenworth, but who were dedicated to the Marines we wanted to save, dedicated to serving our country without payment for the duty we performed. We only wanted to live and love each other like other people. That was part of Matt's wish. I remembered that first night in Hong Kong when he talked about what he wanted in life:

"I so want to find someone to travel through life with. I wish, I wish..." He didn't finish the sentence then either.

He never got what he wished for.

———— • ————

I left Vietnam two weeks later. KC, Don and I went home together just as we had arrived, as if the movie of my life was being played in reverse. There were tears when I said goodbye to these men. Tears when I said goodbye to Joe and LeBlanc. And private tears at night when I was alone.

I was tired and went home to sleep on Hank's parents' couch like I'd done when my mother died.

I soon became bored and reported to San Diego to start laboratory technician school early. I could not stand to be with civilians. My old friends were strangers to me. The only family I had now was the Navy, and I reported back to duty alone and wishing for so much.

CHAPTER FOURTEEN

New Assignment

I was billeted in barracks that held corpsmen training as laboratory technicians. The school was part of the sprawling campus that included the U.S. Naval Hospital Balboa, the Hospital Corps School, and other training disciplines that filled out the Navy's medical needs. It was the largest naval medical education facility in the world. The setting was beautiful, set on the edge of the large park in the middle of San Diego that included the world-class San Diego Zoo, which was located across the street from the campus.

I had been here for my Corps School training so it was familiar. I made friends with an old salt who still lived in the barracks although he was already a tech. I had some beers with him at the EM club one night shortly after arriving.

"So give me the skinny, how long is my training going to be?" I asked.

"There's nine months of training ahead of you, sailor. That's why the Navy extracted another two years off your life." He was a 3rd Class Petty Officer and explained why I needed to up my enlistment from four years to six to get this training.

"That's a long time," I said, "but I'm really interested in science and looking forward to this. What are some of the classes?"

He gave me the textbook explanation. "Eighty percent classroom and the rest is practical experience. That experience will happen in the main lab here at Balboa and the blood bank. You'll spend a lot of your time doing real work. Your classes will include clinical chemistry, hematology, parasitology, and urinalysis. You'll also learn blood donor center operations, specimen processing, laboratory operations, basically management stuff."

I began studies. A class book explained that as a member of the laboratory personnel team, I would examine and analyze body fluids and cells. We would learn to look for bacteria, parasites, and other microorganisms; analyze the chemical content of fluids; match blood for transfusions; and test for drug levels in the blood that would show how a patient was responding to treatment.

I'd also prepare specimens for examination, count cells, and look for abnormal cells in blood and body fluids. I was really looking forward to learning to use high-powered microscopes and other lab equipment. True automated systems were not available and a lot of the work was manual in nature. Gas spectrometers still required making diluted mixtures to measure gas levels in red blood cells.

But while I was anxious to learn, I was having problems with depression and isolation. I missed The Group.

It was difficult being gay when I came back to the U.S. There was a truth combatants knew—with death always hovering close by as a possibility, life meant more. Being gay was easy because you could be gone in a blast. Every moment is vivid in war. I felt more alive in Vietnam. Everything was heightened when I was there, the good times, the quiet times, and the fun crazy times. Sadness and death, especially of Matt, was profound and shattering. The real world both annoyed and bored me. I had no guiding rudder. The loss of Matt had somehow disconnected me completely from life.

I began to hate, really hate, things in my existence. I saw my sister once; she had another baby on the way from a different man than her first child's father. I realized her life was out of control and I didn't want to be part of it. She was living in deep poverty, and selfishly I did not want to give my money to her. I wanted to live for myself, not for her. Sadly, the children she would have would suffer by not having me there.

I began to hate both my father and my mother. It was bizarre for they could do nothing to me now, but I hated them. They had screwed up so much, and my father's condemnation of me was so powerful that I began to question if I wanted to be gay. I really wanted to be normal, and I did not act on my gayness while in school in San Diego.

I made no friends although good people were studying with me. Audrey, a WAVE working toward being a lab tech, was very nice to me. She was from Zanesville, Ohio, and had a twin sister, who was also in the Navy and stationed with us at Balboa.

"I have tickets to see The Association," she told me one day. "We're all going and want you to join us."

I went. It was a great concert in a small hall inside Balboa Park. It was a special performance for the servicemen and women at the hospital and we had front row seats. But none of these people connected with me like those on the *Repose*. I couldn't talk to them, and, by extension, they couldn't help my depression.

At one point, I went to Oak Knoll Naval Hospital in Oakland to see Don. KC was stationed at Camp Lejeune in South Carolina, but Don was relatively close by. I had four days off. We had a great time seeing San Francisco together just like we'd done before going to Vietnam.

He had duty before I was to leave, so I went alone one day to the Haight Ashbury district. The hippies I spoke to in Golden Gate Park were hostile to me. My haircut and civilian clothing gave me away.

"Hey man, you sold out by going in, man. I mean, if we all do what hippies are doing, there would be no more war," a flower-child guy told me.

He was in a dream world. I had already learned that it wasn't a perfect planet. If I had not gone into the service, some poor guy would have taken my place. I just couldn't do that. However, I won him over as a friend because I agreed with him on what crap the war was.

"I've seen how it's wasting the lives of young men. I also know that nothing is going to change," I said.

He asked if I wanted to trip. He had some LSD and he and his friends were all getting ready "to drop." I agreed. I was depressed and he claimed the drug would change my life. At first it was marvelous, the colors and sounds, the euphoria. Plus I was hearing some of the best music being made at the time. It was great. But it lasted too long. I became paranoid after about five hours, and I really wanted to come down. I became desperate. My depression came back with a vengeance on this crap.

When I finally landed from the LSD nine hours later, I decided I never wanted to visit that fake world again. It meant nothing and solved nothing. Plus, when I brought up the subject of gay men, the guy went off.

"A bunch of perverts! Mental degenerates, that's what I think of them fags. Some communes have 'em but none of my friends have anything to with those animals."

So much for free love, I thought. Hippies are homophobes, too.

I returned to San Diego, back to my classes and studies. I was depressed as hell, and anger gripped me around the stomach every waking moment. I didn't understand what was happening to me.

Events of the day would intrude on our life while in lab school. The killing of Martin Luther King Jr. happened in April 1968, then the evening of June 6, one of the guys in my class came into my cubicle in the EM barracks.

"Hey David, get up. Come up to our meeting room next to the main lab. Bobby Kennedy has been shot."

Another assassination of a person that I admired. It compounded my depression even if I had no personal connection with these political figures. They were important in my life. It seemed the world was spinning out of control. My melancholy was so deep I could not concentrate on my studies.

I was having hallucinations, what I dubbed walking nightmares. As I went through the halls or paths of Balboa, I would see dead men floating a foot off the ground horizontally. The men were burned, or bloody with amputations of arms and legs. I found myself unable to control these thoughts. Sleep became impossible, not so much because of dreams, but I would wake with a start because I thought I heard screaming. Screaming wounded.

I couldn't study. To get by in class, I cheated, constantly. I jimmied the fire door of the main office of the tech-school professors at four in the morning, sneaked in and swiped the test sheets they had prepared for each exam. My cheating further enhanced doubt in my abilities and myself. I was a fraud, and like my father had said, I hated myself.

I was so possessed by guilt that I went to the lieutenant in charge of the program.

"Sir, I wish to resign my participation in laboratory technician school."

"Why? Are you unhappy here? Has something happened that you want to talk about?" Lt. Marks asked as I stood before him.

I offered no explanation and was adamant to the point that he relented and allowed me to drop out of lab tech school on August 20, 1968. I accepted the fact that I would still need to fulfill my commitment of a six-year enlistment.

Lt. Marks went to the trouble of finding an obscure NEC on the books of the Navy for a laboratory assistant rating. So I remained a lab tech, but not with the title or pay that would have gone with a full rating.

I couldn't separate the war from The Group. Nothing fed my ego or strengthened me like the work I did in Vietnam and the gay men I worked with. Without them, it was impossible for me to find myself and so I failed miserably in my training. I thought I didn't want to be gay. I was a loser with no strength to lift myself up.

Still, I had learned a lot and was good at doing many procedures despite the fact that I was a cheater. Lt. Marks was a generous man who was completely baffled by my actions. But I could not continue the lie I was perpetrating. I had lost all confidence in myself.

CHAPTER FIFTEEN

Looking for
The Group

Bobby Sponder was at Bethesda Naval Hospital in Maryland and Joe Zielonski was at the National Institutes of Health, right across the street from the hospital. So I asked for an assignment in the D.C. area, hoping to reconnect with the men I spent such an important time in my life with.

My orders came. I was assigned to be a lab assistant in a small clinic at Bainbridge Naval Training Center in Maryland. I reported on September 1, 1968 and made plans to reach Bobby and Joe. I had also found out that Tom had been assigned to St Alban's Naval Hospital in Queens, New York, so he was also not that far away.

When I reported to Bainbridge, I ran into a guy I knew in high school, Dave Forty. He had joined the Navy a year after I did and was in training there.

"I've been here a month taking Radio School," which he called "Beep Beep School." "I have a car and drive up to Philadelphia often. You can get to New York easy from there."

Through him I had transportation to Philly, then I could hop a train to New York. It only took me a few weeks in my new assignment before I visited Tom.

He greeted me warmly. "I'm so glad to see you. I want you to have a great time. Let's paint the Big Apple a new shade of red."

Tom was so alive and well that it brightened me immediately. Once I'd settled into his barracks in Queens, we went into Manhattan.

"We're going to the East Village. There's a great bar I want to take you to. It's called the Stonewall Inn, and it's the best."

Greenwich Village was a magical place. For once in my life I was in a world where just about everyone around me was the same. I didn't feel like an outer spaceman and with Tom, one of my best friends, I had someone who knew the same things I knew, who had the same memories I had. My depression lifted.

As we were coming out of the subway station on Seventh Avenue he listed the rules.

"The bar is owned by the mafia. You'll be paying a charge to get in and you have to buy two drinks minimum. I'm sure that won't be a problem." We both laughed. "But you need to watch out. If you sit at the bar, you must not face sitting outward. Keep your knees to the bar and facing the bartender. Also, sometimes there's a real girl in there. If you want to dance with a guy, ask the girl and the guy can join you on the floor. But no close dancing with the guy is allowed, no touching, okay? Also the drag queens are the greatest people but stay away from them. If we get raided, you'll get into big trouble just by being with them."

I halted midstride. "Raided? What the fuck?" I said.

"Yeah. Sometimes the mafia boss owner is fighting over protection money with the cops. That's when NYPD will come and arrest us. It happens all the time. Plus, there are undercover guys watching so they use these laws of conduct as excuses for arresting us, like the facing-to-the-bar rule."

"Why can't we face outward at the bar?" Frustration and anger rose in my voice.

"That's 'cause they don't want us cruising each other." Tom said. "They do routine sweeps of the bar about once a month even if the cops are paid. They like to fuck with us all the time. It's shit, but that's our life for now."

"Okay. But why stay away from the queens?"

"Because they always get arrested in one of these raids. If you're with them, you automatically go to jail with them for public indecency. The queens are a lot of fun. But it's not worth jail. If the Navy finds out, and they will, you'll end up in Rikers Island for sure."

Tom finished his lecture and we entered the Stonewall Inn.

I sensed that my life had changed. I could see a possibility for us. Not exactly what I was looking for, not what Matt had been looking for, but a place where we could be open and free for just a little while. At Stonewall, which I visited many times, I learned about campiness and I loved the bitchy repartee that went on between us kindred souls.

On October 1, Tom was reassigned to Boston Naval Hospital because he was mustering out of the Navy and asked to finish his enlistment near home, Lewiston, Massachusetts. Boston was the closest duty station. He called and asked me to visit. He wanted to see me one last time. He had something to tell me.

I took the Greyhound to Grand Central Station in New York from Bainbridge, then caught a train to Boston. When I arrived, I again stayed with him at the naval hospital, but this time we did not go out. As we sat in the chow hall he spoke quietly to me.

"I'm getting out in a few weeks and it's been a great run being with you and The Group, but I have to stop this life," he said.

"What do you mean? Seriously, what are you talking about?" I had a dreadful feeling about what he was going to say.

"I'm giving up this life, both the Navy life and the gay life." As my face registered shock and pain, he continued. "Look, there's a woman back home in Lewiston that I promised to marry a long time ago. I see no future in being gay. I want to become a nurse and have a decent life. I cannot see how I can do this by doing men. It's been a blast, but I'm not a kid anymore."

I stayed for only three nights. We did nothing more than have meals together on base. I became depressed again. I couldn't even wrap my head around his idea that what we were, what I was, was kid stuff. If Tom, the rock of our group, wasn't happy, then what hope was there for me?

Since Tom wasn't interested in going out, I went out by myself one night. I walked into Jacques', a seedy gay dive in central Boston. It had what was known as rough trade--joy boys and drag queens, the lowlife of the homosexual underground, according to the straight world. I must have said something about looking for a different kind of place to the bartender. I was in "regulation civvies," which set me apart in this crowd.

"What you're looking for is the bar down the street, The Other Side," the bartender said.

The Other Side was a typical long bar with stools. Three guys sat at the bar, plus the bartender. It was so empty it looked freaky. The bartender at Jacques' told me to order a drink, finish it, then get up and walk to the back of the bar and go through a curtain.

I followed his instructions and found myself standing in front of two heavy, floor-length dark green velvet curtains hanging from a rounded rod. I parted them and entered to find a door in front of me. I opened it and stepped into a dark phone-booth-sized space dimly lit with a red light. Opposite was another door with no doorknob. As I waited, I had the sense of entering a speakeasy during the Prohibition. In a second, the opposite door opened to The Other Side.

I was reminded of the scene in "The Wizard of Oz" when Dorothy opens the front door of her home and sees Munchkin Land in color. Twinkly lights filled a large room, and the ceilings were thirty-feet tall. A stage hunkered on the right, and coming out of the stage, a short runway protruded into the table area. It looked like a thirties' cabaret in the Weimar Republic style.

Magical.

The joint was packed, noisy and smoky with what I guessed to be perhaps a hundred people, mostly men, but some women also. I heard piped-in music, although shows and such were obviously offered as well. Maybe drag? The room held forty small round tables each with four bentwood chairs with curlicues in the back work. Smart tartan covered the seats, attached with round brass brads. The chairs were jumbled. I realized that people had scooted across the floor to join other groups while seated. The configuration changed constantly.

Opposite the secret door was a very long wooden bar that looked right out of the Civil War. It was fashioned of rounded dark wood, deep deep brown with a patina for days. It was empty except for two bartenders and a woman who sat alone at one end. She looked familiar. I realized with a start that it was Judy Garland. No one had noticed her, as far as I could tell.

I stood for a few minutes surveying the room, but I knew I was going to go stand next to Judy. I weaved my way through the tables and chairs and leaned on the bar next to her.

The bartender walked up. "Whatcha having?"

"Scotch and soda, and give the lady another of what she's drinking on me," I said.

The bartender looked at Judy. She nodded and said with a smile, "Make mine a double." Then she winked at me.

Our drinks came and Judy held hers up to toast.

"Where you stationed, sailor?" she asked.

I was not wearing my uniform, not in a gay bar. There were spies in all our bars looking for "criminals" frequenting these "faggot" joints.

"How'd you know I was Navy?" I asked.

"Your hair," Judy replied. "I can recognize the difference from a sailor's haircut and a Marine's. I can also tell if you're in the Army. It's easy once you pay attention. Besides, with all the young men wearing their hair like those Beatle guys, it's not hard to know you're military."

"I'm stationed at Bainbridge, Maryland. I'm a corpsman there, mostly assisting D&Cs. I call them dusting-and-cleaning."

She smiled. "How exactly does that happen?"

I laughed. "It happens because Bainbridge is a basic training center for women who join the Navy. The WAVEs might miss a period or two. The doctors assigned me and other corpsmen to assist in the D&C procedure. Some of the women are pregnant, but it's so early that the D&C fixes it quickly with no danger."

"I see, and this keeps you busy all the time?"

"No. I'm the lab technician for the small lab there. I do basic blood and urinalysis. If more complex stuff needs to be done, I send the specimen up to the Naval Hospital in Philly."

Judy Garland looked me in the eye. "Seen action?"

"'Nam. I just got back from a tour. I don't understand what's happening there, but I went and I'm glad I went. I took care of the boys."

"Some of the best times of my life were doing USO shows. Do you know the only real people in the world are military men? Everyone else is a big phony. The military boys, they love my music. And I love them. Genuine, know what I mean?"

I nodded. "I do, kinda hard for the lavender guys but we manage. Gays are coming out, you know?"

"My best audiences. I'm going to London in a few days. I laugh at myself because the Brit men all sound like poufs to me. But I know my gays will be in the audience, and I've decided this is going to be the best show I've ever given. My comeback."

I laughed. "You got panned by the critics for the last concert."

Judy shrugged. "Too much booze and pills. I'm better, but when I travel to foreign countries I really have trouble sleeping. So the pills, well, they help and they hurt."

"I like this place. It's not seedy like most," I said, to change the subject.

"I like it because no one bothers me here. I can have a quiet drink and no big deal with these guys. Respect. They have respect. Only my gays." She seemed sad, but also both beautiful and fragile. She reminded me of my mother.

"I have to go," I said. "But I don't catch the train for New York City until late tomorrow. You want to have dinner or something?"

"Yes, but they don't let me eat. I'm half-starved all day. But we can meet tomorrow. There's a little alley around the corner called Carver Street. A small restaurant there called Twelve Carver knows me. May we meet there?"

I wondered who "they" were that didn't let her eat. But I didn't push it. We arranged to meet at six. As I got up to leave, she touched my arm. She winked again, held up her cocktail and made a little clinking move with it.

Carver Street was only a block long. Two colonial-style street lamps gave off the yellow carbon filament light of the olden days. It had rained and sleeted all day. In the dark, the street shined brightly with little patches of ice crystals piled against the curb. The year could have been 1800.

The restaurant was small; a cute gay couple stepped out. One was holding his friend's cape for him to slip on. Capes were in that year.

All the gay boys wore them, and they looked even smarter in their Bass Weeguns. The look was called preppy, the word originating from the university preparatory schools located in and around Boston.

The large paned windows on each side of the entry of Twelve Carver were oddly wavy. I guessed it was original colonial glass. The lamps inside had Tiffany-style covers and cast an amber light through the window. I could see Judy sitting in the window seat on the right. It was like seeing through the bottom of a Coke bottle. She looked gossamer, dreamy.

"Good evening, Miss Garland. Really nice seeing you again," I said as I sat. I was wearing my blues, thirteen buttons, tight pants.

"Thank you, my sailor. Really, it's just good to see you, I like talking with you."

"When I was hitting the camps during World War II, I remember the boys always had nicknames for each other. What's yours?"

"I was called Bac Si or Bac Si Joe in Vietnam. That's the only nickname I ever had. The Vietnamese kids called me that when I entered a village during a county fair day in the field. We did minor medical stuff for the children. I think it means 'doctor,' but I don't know. It stuck. My buddies called me 'Boxie.'"

"Well, Boxie, I like that. If you don't mind, I'll use that." I nodded. "Like I said yesterday, my best days were during the war. Sad, really, but there you are. Like you, I can't understand the war. It is the men who are fighting this conflict that concern me the most. I think of them. I saw something sad in your eyes yesterday. Was it tough for you?"

"It was very tough. I saw and did things that I wasn't ready for. I have visions and dreams that have me on edge a lot. But it wasn't all bad. I had a group of gay buddies who held me together. Well, we held each other together. But…"

I stopped talking at that moment as I thought of Matt.

"But one of them died?"

We looked at each other and she knew the answer.

We ordered dinner and chatted more about my Navy experiences. I had duck confit on a bed of greens. Judy had a salad, but all she ate were two croutons. The rest, the tomatoes and lettuce, she moved around the plate like chessmen on a board.

She didn't talk much about herself. I didn't probe and made small talk instead. Like the time I saw Martha Raye in a show in Nam. Judy and I laughed loudly as I told her one of Raye's off color jokes and how much it embarrassed me. Judy agreed that Raye could be pretty salty, or as Judy put it, "a real truck-stop Tess."

The evening ended quickly. We didn't exchange addresses. It wasn't that kind of thing. As I stood to leave, Judy Garland pulled me down and planted a small kiss on my cheek.

"I can tell you're not happy with being gay. Find a cause you want to fight for in the community. Get a purpose as a gay man and you'll be happier. I know for myself, I have lost that in my art. I hope to find it or die for the trying. You must find something or someone, and soon."

I walked out into Carver Street and felt the chill in the air. One of the cape-wearing gay guys was standing under a yellow light smoking a cigarette. Suddenly, it was as if Sherlock Holmes was standing there and Jack the Ripper was hiding in the shadows. I can't say I had a premonition. I just remember feeling that something bad was going to happen.

Judy Garland died on June 22, 1969. Her funeral was held on June 28 at 11 a.m. in New York City. It was hot and humid, but huge crowds showed up inside the church and outside. On the evening of the funeral, the Stonewall riots began when the police did one of their 2 a.m. raids that Tom had told me about. The riots would last almost three days.

It had been such a sad day for gays. I felt the tragedy of Judy's life mirrored in what I was going through as a gay man. I think that affected everyone's mood in the Stonewall, so when the police busted the place for the umpteenth time, they went nuts. They'd had it with the harassment.

I didn't participate in the riots. But a few weeks later, I was in New York again. I took a walk up Madison Avenue past Campbell's Funeral Home on 82nd. A uniformed doorman stood at the front. I wondered if he was there during Judy's funeral. I crossed Madison and asked him.

His voice took on a reverent tone, nearly religious. "Everyone worked on the day of Miss Garland's funeral. No one would take the day off—our staff was at full capacity that day because of the crowds."

"I remember seeing a photo in the Daily News. It was of the family leaving the funeral. Liza's out in front, holding Lorna's hand. Kay Thompson has her hands around Lorna's shoulders, and Peter Allen is in the back with his hands on Kay and Lorna's shoulders."

I didn't need to ask him the rest of my question. He turned and pointed to a private side door of the funeral home.

"That photo was taken right there. We brought the children out the side door to avoid the crowds in the front." Suddenly I felt the weight of Judy Garland's death on the gay subculture. I was seeing signs of heavy drug use among gays in New York and it worried me. I wish I could tell them no more pills. I wish I had told Judy the same.

Before tears could form in my eyes, I said a hurried goodbye and ran down Madison Avenue.

My sadness and depression had worsened with the loss of Tom as a gay ally. Now with Judy Garland's death, I was thinking of suicide.

CHAPTER SIXTEEN

The End

In January 1969 I received orders out of Bainbridge. The Navy was sending me to the Education Center at the Marine base in Quantico, Virginia. Since I was reporting to new duty with the Marines, I changed into my Marine green-machine uniform again. I would be close to Bobby and Joe. I was hoping they could help me out of my depression.

I handed my orders to the chief that I was told to report to after checking in with the personnel office. He told me he'd been working alone at the clinic lab for over a year.

"You, my friend, are going to get me three weeks liberty," he said.

"Happy to help, Chief. Give me the rundown," I said.

My duties would be the same as at Bainbridge, basic blood, and urine and bacterial cultures. More difficult stuff would go to the tiny Navy hospital on base. I was in the small health clinic to take care of everyday illnesses and the physicals that were necessary at Quantico, a large training center for Marines and FBI personnel. There was also a small flight school for Marines who thought they could be Navy pilots so they came to get checked out physically.

As I'd hoped, being near some of The Group worked in taking me out of my depressive state. Bobby and Joe were sharing an apartment on Battery Lane just off Wisconsin Avenue, three blocks from

Bethesda Naval Hospital in Maryland and about the same distance from the NIH, where they worked. Quantico was a short train ride to Maryland, so I rejoined this small portion of The Group, which now included Bob LeBlanc, the Marine we got to know in Singapore who took care of Matt's body when he died. Bob was stationed at the Marine barracks in Virginia, just across the Potomac from D.C.

"Have you found the best gay bars in the city?" I asked the first weekend I went to spend with them.

"The Hideaway and the Georgetown Grill are the best places. The Hideaway has dancing and the Georgetown Grill is just down Wisconsin Avenue, so the bus takes us there and brings us back anytime we want," Bobby said.

I asked how the harassment laws were, as I was curious about the dancing.

"That's only in New York. Those mafia-run bars and crooked cops don't have a chance here. Too many politicians and high-ranking military queer guys going to these joints, so no problems like that. You're going to love it here."

Love it I did. Our group took to meeting nice older gay men who had fancy homes in Georgetown and would pay for our drinks and dinners. They were successful men and we attended swanky parties in their charming homes. I was under no illusions. Basically they were paying us for sex. But who doesn't pay for sex? What do you call that diamond women insist on getting if marriage is proposed? I made sure my men, who we called "tricks" in the fashion of prostitutes, were handsome as well as rich, and I used my uniform to snare them.

In April an off-Broadway play that had made a sensation in New York was coming to Washington. One of our gentlemen friends bought us military guys tickets to see it. The play was "The Boys in the Band" and it would open at Ford's Theater in D.C. Ford's was a legitimate playhouse with a long history, including the fact that it was where John Wilkes Booth assassinated President Abraham Lincoln. "Boys in the Band" was the first gay-themed play of our time and we were dying to see it.

"My my my," said Joe fanning himself theatrically as we entered the hall. "There are just too many old men and boy toys. A tad obvious if you ask me."

Bobby, LeBlanc and I tittered like Jane Austen characters at Joe's observation.

The play was amazing. As I watched, I saw the self-deprecating humor our Group used. I knew exactly where that came from. The dialogue and storyline was mean and developed from a place of pain in the characters' lives. I realized I was living this play. The central character of a fag with low self-esteem resonated with me. I began to sense that my feelings about myself were coming from what society told me about myself. It was external judgment that made us gay guys hate ourselves.

In the play, a fight takes place between one of the characters and a straight guy, maybe closeted. It was not too long before The Group went to a party where the scene played out in real life. The perpetrator at our party was a bitchy mean fag named Marvin Hall. He was a Navy dental tech stationed in Quantico. I hated him. He was a terrible person and dangerous, but impossible to avoid because he ran in the same circles we did.

Marvin became angry with his trick's cousin for trying to break them up. I couldn't blame the cousin. Marvin was a user in the worst sense of the word. He started a catfight that ended in slaps and slammed doors. The Group sat on the hallway stairs, laughing at the fool among us. Not everything that came with Marvin was terrible, however. He worked with another dental tech, Drew, who wasn't gay but we became friends, despite his knowing that I was. We hung out a lot together on base.

"Hey, you want to get high?" Drew asked one day.

"I'm really not into the hippie thing. I love the music, but that acid shit does not sit well with me. It makes me sick, both physically and mentally." I told him about the miserable trip I had in San Francisco.

"Hell no, not LSD," said Drew. "Pot. I have some great pot and it is nothing like LSD. It's fun and only lasts a couple of hours. Not like the nine-hour trip you had."

That weekend I checked out a jeep from the Marine motor pool at Quantico. I had access because I'd been in combat and the Marines gave me whatever I wanted.

"Let's go out to Lunga Lake. It's really beautiful, and with the weather so hot, we can jump in the lake to cool off and smoke our asses off," Drew suggested.

I was so happy being friends with Drew because it was the first time I got to know a straight man who was so sure of his own masculinity that he was not intimidated or hostile to me.

Drew was right. Marijuana was a wonderful drug that should never have been made illegal. We got into a crazy laughing jag and fell into each other's arms at one point. He kissed me on the mouth. As I looked at him in surprise, he said, "Don't get the wrong idea. We're not getting into the sack together. But you're such a sweet guy and I really like you. I just wanted to kiss you."

"You're fucking high," I said, and laughed. "Now leave me alone or I'll report you."

Drew turned serious. "Speaking of reporting, watch out for Marvin. He has a big mouth and I think he's responsible for a gay guy getting kicked out a few months back. I'm sure it was Hall who told CID about the kid being gay. The boy was put in the brig and given a dishonorable discharge."

CID was the Criminal Investigation Department of the Marines. One crime high on their list was the ferreting out of queers in the military. CID men were dangerous and persistent.

"Have you heard about the Atlantic City Pop Festival?" Drew asked two days later after our afternoon together. "It starts August 1 at the Atlantic City racetrack. They're going to have Iron Butterfly and a bunch of other groups. I just got my VW bus fixed so I want to ride up to New Jersey and hear the music. We can sleep in the VW so it won't cost us anything for motels."

I agreed immediately. We would spend three nights listening to some of the best music of the time. We smoked pot and heard The Chambers Brothers, who followed Iron Butterfly. As the Chambers started playing "Time Has Come Today," I jumped onto one of the huge speakers on the stage. It was so large I could literally dance around on it. I developed a lifelong hearing loss because of that but I didn't care.

Drew woke me our second morning. "Little Richard is filling in for Johnny Winter, and look it—can you believe this, they're setting up a white, grand piano. Come on, let's go dancing!"

I flew out of the VW and we rocked out with the craziest act I had ever seen. That weekend we also got to hear Janis Joplin sing with her musicians, the Full-Tilt Boogie Band, which backed her as she sang, "Try." She also did a cover of The Chantels' "Maybe" and "As Good As You've Been to This World." She even joined Little Richard on stage for a few tunes.

Drew and I sat smoking and talking on our last night. "I think I like Joe Cocker the most," I said. "The songs 'With A Little Help From My Friends' and 'Feelin' Alright' are probably the most soulful things I've heard in my life. Do you think he sings with such passion because he's spastic?" I was so loaded that I had that impression because he did these weird moves with his hands as if playing an air guitar.

Drew doubled over laughing so hard that he almost threw up. "You fucktard, that's just how he sings. He's not spastic."

I loved Drew. His humor and honesty were something I hoped I could find in a partner someday.

The entire time people were talking about an even bigger event being planned that would take place in upstate New York, where some guy had rented out his farm for a days-long music festival. People were so jazzed about what we saw at Atlantic City that everyone said they were going.

"I would love to hit that scene," I said. "But man, I shot my liberty-wad to hell and back."

Drew had no time for it either. So we missed out on Woodstock. The news reported that over a half million crazed hippies, and probably a bunch of military men, descended on the area, which turned it into a disaster zone.

The rest of August 1969 took a downward turn. The peaceniks staged a big antiwar rally in Washington D.C. Our Marine unit at Quantico was sent to guard the Capitol. We loaded into military vehicles to head north in a convoy. I could not help but remember fifties' science fiction movies that always had troops convoying into the capital to attack the aliens. But these people were not aliens.

They were conscientious people who believed that what the United States was doing in Vietnam was a tragedy for everyone involved. The people of Vietnam would never be changed from their communist ways and our boys were being killed for nothing. Some of them had begun to attack us servicemen as if it were our fault that the war continued. We were called "baby killers" and taunted in public. I had no animosity toward them; they were just scared. Their fear was real. The draft was still happening, and the useless killing was still going on, on both sides.

Bobby and I tried to make light of what was happening. He jumped into the back of the truck and announced "Dumfries own," a reference we'd heard in old World War II movies to describe a small town's boys going off to war together. Dumfries was a village just outside the base at Quantico.

We spent a night in the rotunda of the Capitol as people rioted outside along the Mall, stretching from the Capitol to the Lincoln Memorial. Bobby and I were dismissed the next day. While he went home, I changed into civvies, grabbed my corpsman medical bag and joined the protesters. I had to. I was one of those conscientious people who hated the war. I wasn't a freak and neither were these protesters. So I went and patched rioters' head wounds, skin abrasions, and cleaned tear gas from eyes.

In mid-October 1969, the bottom fell out of my life. I was summoned by the commanding officer of the Marines at Quantico who directed me to report to OSI, the Office of Special Investigation, a CID unit. I sat in a small room, where I waited for what seemed like hours. Finally, a man dressed in civilian clothes came in and introduced himself as a special agent of the OSI. He said allegations had been made against me.

"What allegations?" I asked.

"You being a faggot," he said.

I knew it was Marvin. He didn't like The Group. He was not a person we wanted. He was a vindictive prig. And so it happened. My military career ended. My years of service in a war zone counted for nothing. My passion for saving the lives of my fellow servicemen counted for even less. I was deemed a leper and was treated as such.

The OSI man said he wanted names and ranks of other homos I knew and that I had to submit to more detailed questioning by other CID agents.

"You will report back here to my office at 0900 tomorrow. Do you understand?"

I walked out of his office in a daze. Then I realized that for the two years since leaving Vietnam I had been in a walking nightmare. I had not been connected to the world that entire time. I was exhausted. The war visions had never really stopped. I had tricked my mind into believing I was okay because of the contact I had with Joe and Bobby. But really I was just as fucked up in my head as I'd been in San Diego.

The news months before that David Monarch had died at Leavenworth had something to do with it. I never learned the facts of his death, the how and why, but in 1960s America, we gay men deserved to die, according to popular thinking. So who cared that a queer black man had died in prison? "What did you expect?" would have been the reply, had I asked anyone.

Threatened with a court-martial that carried a sentence of nineteen months in the federal prison at Ft. Leavenworth along with a dishonorable discharge, I was filled with terror at the prospect of dying like David Monarch.

I might as well die now, I thought, under my own terms.

At two in the morning I went to my small laboratory. The medical bottles, beakers and Bunsen burners looked frightening in the small light I'd turned on. Frankenstein's lab, I thought. I removed the burner, leaving the tubing attached to the gas valve. Fitting a large plastic bag, I punched the tube through the closed end and taped around the tube and plastic, making it as leak proof as I could. I pulled up one of the lab's high stools to the counter and slipped my head into the open end of the plastic bag. Using more tape, I tightened the bag around my neck achieving a good seal.

I turned on the gas to fill the bag. I then turned it off and lay my head on the granite top and shut my eyes.

Was it the war? Was it the harassment for being gay? I didn't know. All I knew was that I felt like the biggest loser on the planet. I hated being gay and I felt I didn't deserve to live.

As the gas replaced the oxygen in my system, my head started spinning and I heard squeaky noises inside my skull. Then I felt even suicide was futile. I pulled the plug on the gas pipe, tore off the bag and sat up.

I didn't want to leave the Navy. It had given tremendous meaning and structure to my life. It had rescued me when I was a lost youth. It had made me a man.

But I knew I had to leave.

I reported to the psychiatrist in my clinic about my suicide attempt. That stopped the legal proceedings in their tracks. Even the U.S. Navy wasn't so cruel as to deny treatment for an obviously mentally disturbed individual.

I spent the following nine months in the psychiatric unit of Bethesda Naval Hospital. When I arrived, they put me on a lockdown ward, specifically in a padded secured room for the violently disturbed. They did not want a dangerous homosexual to be in the general patient population before they evaluated my condition. I was given large, intramuscular doses of Thorazine, a potent psychotropic drug, for a time.

Bobby, Joe, and LeBlanc visited me once while I was at Bethesda, but I think I frightened them. As much as I needed their comfort, because my physical condition was terrible, they demurred from seeing me again. Thorazine had a terrible effect on me. I was unable to walk properly because the drug messed with my motor skills. I exhibited the "Thorazine shuffle," short jerky steps, when I came out to the visiting area where The Group waited to see me. I saw the horror in their eyes. I suspected they had fears about themselves and their future. They had looked up to me once. Here, I was a broken man, a failure.

Finally, my doctor lifted my lockdown status, stating in my chart that I was not a sexual threat to other psychiatric patients. In fact, he diagnosed me as only experiencing a homosexual panic condition. He wrote I wasn't really a homosexual, but recommended my discharge anyway.

I received a general discharge under less than honorable conditions. I never officially learned who my accuser was. I assumed it was Marvin, but in the service, I had no rights, and they refused to divulge that information. However, I never confirmed that I had sex with men, and they couldn't prove I was gay. The military judged me a homosexual criminal despite the lack of real evidence and the psychiatrist's diagnosis. My DD214 discharge document contained two codes that would mark me for life: 265, unsuitability because of a character disorder, and 256, homosexual, acceptance of discharge in lieu of board action, the prison sentence.

I packed my sea bag for the last time, although I would not take it or the uniforms I had loved so much with me. I turned them into the supply store. The only things I kept were Matt's Marine sweatshirt and his Zippo. But I couldn't keep my own uniforms. The Navy had disappointed me. At the last second, though, I kept my peacoat. I couldn't find it in myself to let go completely of my time in the service, of this period in my life that had shaped me. I walked out of Bethesda Naval Hospital in civilian clothes and took a taxi directly to Arlington National Cemetery. There I consulted the graves locater man.

"I'm looking for the USS *Forrestal* crew member sites, and Matt Horn, a Navy corpsman KIA'd in Vietnam."

He thumbed through his logs and found Matt's site. He gave me a map on which he marked the location of his grave. It was quite close, just up Memorial Drive to Memorial Stadium, and to the right in Area 13.

"Son, the *Forrestal* has a special monument for the fallen from the fire aboard her. It's a group burial site for eighteen sailors, near the Tomb of the Unknown Soldier." He explained that it was important not to confuse a group burial with an unknown. "In a group burial, the individuals are known, but because of the circumstances of their deaths, they are individually unidentifiable," he explained.

I remembered one of the dead I worked so hard to try and identify. His burned body was missing the lower jaw. I tried to plot the upper teeth, but they were too damaged to get a proper diagram. He would be there. I was anxious to pay my respects to him and all the men I and my fellow sailors got home that day.

I took a taxi to the memorial. On it, each sailor's name and personal data were engraved. The date of their death was at the bottom of the list of names: USS *Forrestal* July 29, 1967. Actually, only fifteen remains were buried there. It was later determined that three sailors had been blown overboard in the initial explosions and their bodies were never found. So the Department of Defense decided to include their names along with the unidentifiable.

I walked the entire distance from the Forrestal Memorial back to Area 13 near the entrance of the cemetery. I stood at Matt's head stone. Rivulets of tears ran down my cheeks.

I couldn't pray. I was never religious. But at that moment I looked to the sky and hoped there was a God and that my Matt was with Him. I spoke the words that I had said that moment when he died. "I wish we could have been lovers. I love you, man. I love you!"

Then I left to start a life that would make his dreams, and mine, come true. A just world for us. I was determined.

EPILOGUE

I stood in the middle of a street in West Hollywood, California. It was September 20, 2011, and gay men and women were dancing in the street around me in a huge raucous celebration.

That day the military ended its "Don't ask, don't tell" policy. Gay men and women could now serve openly in the United States Armed Services. It was a monumental day for gay civil rights.

Overcome with emotion, I cried my soul out, there on the street. I felt joy because people like me would never again have to go through what I went through. And I was brokenhearted because the change came too late for me and my peers.

After leaving the service, I became successful. Despite being classified as having a low IQ, like the mentally retarded savant able to memorize the telephone book, I had a gift. I understood the digital world and computer software the moment it came into the American business world. I actually became a leader at AT&T in propelling the networks and software that drive everything we do today. I am comfortably retired because of my talents and because of my service to my country.

I lived my life as an openly gay man. In all the jobs I had after my military service, I made sure everyone knew who my true self was. Never again was I going to be closeted. People had to deal with me as I was, and my openness helped overcome prejudices.

I went even further and became a gay rights activist. In 1971, I helped start the Gay Community Service Center in Los Angeles. It is now the LGBT Center of Los Angeles, one of the largest and most successful such organizations in the country. During the AIDS crisis I joined the AIDS Coalition to Unleash Power, or ACT-UP, the organization that pushed the establishment to find treatments to stop the disease ravaging the gay community. I also joined the Names Project AIDS Memorial Quilt, a memorial designed to show the world that those of us dying are human beings with lives and loves that deserved honoring.

Three decades after I returned from Vietnam, however, the war that I had stuffed deep inside me rushed back with a vengeance. I now know I lived my entire life with PTSD, but it took President George W. Bush and his war on Iraq to push me over the edge.

On March 20, 2003, as I watched television reports of the U.S. invasion, Vietnam played before my eyes. I knew instinctively that the president was lying about weapons of mass destruction to justify the war in Iraq, as presidents in the sixties and seventies had used the threat of Communism to justify American involvement in the war in Vietnam. I knew that the gases Saddam Hussein had used against minority citizens of his country were not produced there, but provided indirectly from chemical companies in the United States, the same companies that poisoned me and the civilians of Vietnam with Agent Orange. I knew that young men (and now women) would be maimed and die for no reason at all. I collapsed into depression, hallucinations and isolation, the hallmark signs of PTSD.

My health suffered as PTSD overtook me, eventually preventing me from continuing my career. My anger and its physical toll caused a cascade of events that drove me to despair.

My partner of fourteen years left me. I so loved him and I still wish we were together, but I know now he did not really love me. If he had, he would have seen I was suffering and helped me recover.

I ended up in a cabin in the woods of far northern California. I hunkered down there alone for the better part of a year. I was paranoid of the world, the lurking unseen enemy so I surrounded the cabin with barbed wire and attached cans so I could hear intruders. I never knew that demons had been hiding in me since I returned from Vietnam.

Eventually, I snapped out of it. I started to write about Vietnam, and by setting words on paper, I found new purpose in life. But it took five years to get control of my PTSD. I did so with the help of a gay doctor at the Veterans Administration. He saved my life.

I have found another new purpose, a final purpose for my being on the planet. While the greater world will not accept us for centuries yet, in the United States we have made great leaps for LGBT people among the country's diverse groups. But there is one last element after marriage equality that needs to be put in place before I am done with my influence in this struggle, and that is how we live as aged LGBT people.

The question must be asked, what will happen to the old gay men of my era who built it all? The advances of age are taking a terrible toll on the end of these lives. Many elderly gay men live an isolated, desolate, and lonely existence. The reality is that eight out of ten of our friends, and what would have been our support structure, died in the 1980s. My generation is still in uncharted waters.

My peers and I tried to make a society and ethos for us as gay men to live by within the straight society. We wanted nothing more than what everyone else had: to be treated fairly and equally. We built that world for ourselves over my lifetime. In no era of mankind have we existed in the way we do now in the United States. My friends and I built it, making mistakes, but also having enormous successes.

The reason we pushed for marriage equality is so the societal structures are in place to allow LGBT individuals to build families and homes. My personal thinking is that the excesses of the 1970s facilitated the spread of AIDS. But the modern era did not give us a roadmap for our lives and relationships. Mistakes were made. We learned and changed. I think credit should be given, not derision.

I write this story to alert the younger generation of queers. They must think about how they want to structure their micro-society for the aged that are coming. Marriage and the community that it builds will hopefully give us new ways of treating each other when we grow old. But the young need to be reminded. This short story of my beginning is my reminder to them.

Over the years, I have tried to track down the other members of The Group. In many ways, they epitomize the life outcomes of gay men of my era.

Bobby was discharged from the Navy at the same time I was. His enlistment was up and he returned home to Ohio. When I first was out of the Navy, I became homeless for almost a year. Living on the road, I crisscrossed the United States in the fashion of a hobo. I hitched rides, jumped trains and slept under bridges. I visited Bobby in Ohio as I headed east from Los Angeles, a vagabond with no place to go. He was polite, but unfriendly. He acknowledged that he was dating an older man in Chicago, but he had no pride in his gayness. He seemed to be enduring it. I never heard from him again. Google searches have come up empty.

In 1987 I was a volunteer taking the Names Project AIDS Memorial Quilt to display on the National Mall in Washington D.C. As I finished my first day's shift, I walked to join the ring of visitors who'd come to see the quilts and remember the dead. As the names echoed over the PA system, I spotted a familiar face, older now by seventeen years.

"Excuse me. Are you Joe Green?"

Joe had once explained that his name meant green in Polish, and I had sometimes called him Joe Green as we ran around together with The Group.

He blinked twice, his face registering recognition. "Is it you, David?"

I nodded. We hugged and cried. We spoke about the quilt and AIDS. His boyfriend had succumbed to the disease just that year. But Joe was a broken man. He talked about turning to God for redemption because surely He was punishing us. I realized he had never embraced his homosexuality with pride. He was like Bobby, enduring his fate and walking through life just to get to the end.

In 2012 I remembered that Tom was from Lewiston, Massachusetts, and using the Internet I did a phone number search on his name. As I called the only Tom Conkin listed in Lewiston, I was hopeful when a woman answered.

"By any chance, was the Tom that owns this telephone in the Navy?"

The woman gasped slightly. "Yes it is. Were you on the USS *Repose?*"

"Tom and I served together. We were the best of buddies during the war. May I speak to him?" I know my voice betrayed my happiness.

"I'm sorry. Tom died in 1998 from a brain aneurysm."

I was crestfallen. Uncomfortably, I found out that she was his widow and they had had two children, who still missed him terribly.

"I remember him as a funny scamp, always quick to joke," I said. "He had a way of standing sideways clutching his hands together like the witch that held the apple for Snow White."

She was laughing before I ended the sentence. "He never changed. I remember that pose. It's so funny to hear you describe it. It makes me happy knowing his Navy friends remember him like I do."

"Did you find among his possessions a Zippo lighter with the words 'The Group' inscribed on it?" I was eager to know if he still remembered us, and his gayness.

She answered quickly that she had found it and then she said the most remarkable thing. "Would you like to have it? I'll send it to you," she said.

I didn't prolong the conversation. I felt awkward after finding out he had abandoned his real self. A couple days later, the lighter arrived in the mail.

Bob LeBlanc lives in Palm Springs, and though he has cancer from his exposure to Agent Orange, he is in remission and doing well. We have remained friends and see each other often. So in that small way, The Group is still together.

In 2019, my life came full circle. Three years before, I was talking to Stephanie Stone, chief deputy director of the Los Angeles County Department of Military and Veterans Affairs. She suggested I consult attorneys doing pro-bono legal assistance to help vets like me petition the Department of Defense to upgrade my discharge from "general under less than honorable circumstances." With their help, I filed my petition, together with an affidavit from the V.A. doctor who treated my combat-related PTSD. On April 29, 2019, the Department of the Navy upgraded my discharge. The official communication said in part:

"Petitioner's record supports that he was administratively discharged on the basis of his homosexuality using a policy similar to DADT, and that there were absolutely no aggravating factors surrounding his discharge. Accordingly, the Board concludes that no useful purpose is served by continuing to characterize the Petitioner's service as having been discharged due to unsuitability and/or a character disorder."

After almost fifty years, I received my Honorable Discharge for service to the United States of America.

When I die, what I think of as the end of the movie of my life, I have asked that three things be put in my casket: Three Zippo lighters, Tom's, Matt's and mine. They will be with me when I finish my journey.

I've also instructed that the Navy hymn be sung at my memorial. I sang this song as a songbird in boot camp and heard it at the funerals of the men who died in Vietnam.

> Almighty Father, strong to save,
> Whose arm hath bound the restless wave,
> Who bidd'st the mighty ocean deep
> Its own appointed limits keep:
> O hear us when we cry to thee
> For those in peril on the sea.

Acknowledgements

I need to acknowledge Bud Gundy for giving me the inspiration to write, the U.S. Veterans' Artists Alliance and its executive director Keith Jeffreys for supporting and encouraging me and my writing, our leader Timothy Wurtz, and Christina Hoag, who edited this book. You all took the helm of my ship and steered it on course.

I acknowledge my life and my memories.

About the Author

Dave Lara is a Mexican-American-Jew born in Castroville, California, to a poor family of migrant workers.

In 1965, at seventeen years of age, he was emancipated and joined the U.S. Navy in the hopes of avoiding duty in the Vietnam War. Eleven months later, he found himself in the jungles of Vietnam where he learned he could be someone of worth.

While he struggled with his homosexuality at first, he went on to be part of the revolution that formed the modern day gay rights movement. His novel *Butterfly Dream*, co-written with Bud Gundy, is the first in a series of four.

———◦———

Dave is available for speaking engagements. If you would like to have Dave speak to your group, please contact the USVAA at www.usvaa.org, using the contact form on the "About" tab.